T0279506

PRAISE FOR
SPHERES OF INFLUENCE

"With this highly readable book as a guide, emerging leaders can swiftly develop the critical career-enhancing skill of relationship building. Page after page offers practical advice and countless concrete examples of how to—and how not to—build and manage strong business relationships. *Spheres of Influence* is a must-read for anyone aspiring to or in a position of leadership."

—Naomi Karten, author of *Managing Expectations: Working with People Who Want More, Better, Faster, Sooner, NOW!*

"This book is a beacon of wisdom for anyone seeking to build meaningful connections and authentic business relationships in the professional world. With actionable insights and genuine, heartfelt advice, it offers a road map to not only cultivate trust and rapport, but also foster enduring partnerships that form the bedrock of successful careers."

—Steve Rohleder, chairman of the board, Cognizant

"*Spheres of Influence* is a wonderful book for emerging leaders. Its practical advice interspersed with real-life stories captivates the reader and culminates in succinct key takeaways at the end of each chapter. Brad's breadth of leadership experience clearly comes through in this book!"

—Pallavi Verma, senior managing director, Accenture

"Brad Englert's *Spheres of Influence* is a fast read and wonderful tutorial on building and sustaining internal and external partnerships with bosses, executive teams, peers, and direct reports. Brad provides numerous references and rich examples of how to understand your partners' goals and aspirations, set and manage their expectations, and genuinely care about their success. I worked with Brad many years ago. Brad is the real deal, and so is *Spheres of Influence.*"

—Edward J. Ray, president emeritus and professor
of economics, Oregon State University

"*Spheres of Influence* brilliantly illustrates that in the game of life, the strongest moves are made through the power of genuine connections. Brad Englert's book is a master class in the art of influence with heart, where relationships reign supreme!"

—Liz Aebersold, founder, Wildcard Thinking

"Brad provides a thoughtful and practical guide to help emerging leaders build effective and enduring business relationships. His views are based on front-line experiences, built over a successful career in consulting and higher education administration. He's walked the walk!"

—Marty Cole, chairman, Sagility Health and Arrivia;
Board Member, Western Union, Western Digital,
and Wilson HCG; former chief executive, Technology
Group, Accenture; and former CEO, Cloudera

"I've worked in higher education, the federal government, and the corporate world, and this book is a must-read for anyone in any of these sectors. Whether it's understanding how to work with your boss or other leaders, or managing your relationships with vendor partners, Brad provides great examples of how to navigate real situations and build trust. And, along the way, you may learn a lot about yourself—how to be a better boss and leader and how to be a better client partner."

—Darcy W. Hardy, PhD, associate vice president for academic affairs and director, Anthology Education and Research Center

"Brad has delivered a master class in managing setbacks, fostering successful business relationships, and building a resilient business culture. His unique approach to problem-solving, underscored by grit and humility, offers a fresh perspective on how to face challenges head-on and emerge stronger. *Spheres of Influence* is not just a book about business; it's a book about the power of the human connection in the world of business."

—Olu Kole-James, director, global client services, VISA

"This book is a survival kit. Make the key takeaways your personal chants. Englert's knowledge and wisdom will be a recurring lifeline as I begin my career in the federal government. The stories serve as valuable lessons of proper conduct and cautionary tales of dos and don'ts. *Spheres of Influence* unlocks personal and professional successes for you, your colleagues, managers, and customers."

—Zane Evans, returned peace corps volunteer and master of global policy studies, LBJ School of Public Affairs, The University of Texas at Austin

"Brad Englert asserts the importance of developing authentic business relationship skills as one would any other hard skill. His clear advice and concise takeaways will put you on the right road to a leadership position."

—Margaret Jabour, executive vice president and
co-owner, Twin Liquors Fine Wine and Spirits

"In *Spheres of Influence*, Brad Englert does a masterful job of helping readers to develop trust with their colleagues and strategic partners by understanding their goals, advancing projects, and ensuring clarity of roles. He illustrates his wisdom with stories drawn from his long and successful career. This book is for anyone who wants to be a more effective communicator and partner in the workplace."

—Art Markman, vice provost for academic affairs
The University of Texas at Austin, contributor,
Fast Company, and author of *Bring Your Brain to Work*

"Brad Englert masterfully weaves his 40 years of experience to create a playbook for professionals of all levels to successfully navigate their business relationships."

—Christy Asyn, software development engineer, Amazon

"Professional relationships have their own set of rules, and can be the make-or-break for your professional success. *Spheres of Influence* will show you how to establish, maintain, and flourish relationships with those you work for and work with."

—David Jabour, president,
Twin Liquors Fine Wine and Spirits

"As technology's influence in the workplace grows, so does the challenge of managing the people it takes to make it work. By weaving together his own extensive experience with that of other experts, Brad Enlgert provides a timely and extremely useful road map on how managers can successfully engage the people they work with and work for."

—William Shkurti, former senior vice president
for business and finance, The Ohio State University

"To become an emerging leader in your field, you need to master the hard skill of building authentic business relationships. Brad Englert shows us how to do that with practical advice, real-world stories, and clear examples. This book is a must-read for anyone who wants to grow their influence, impact, and income in the business world."

—Dennis Passovoy, assistant professor of
management, McCombs School of Business,
The University of Texas at Austin

"Go network!" they say. But how? In *Spheres of Influence*, Brad leaves no space for fluff and breaks down what you can do right now to not just "network," but to transform strangers into allies and skeptics into believers. Useful no matter where you are in your career."

—Gorick Ng, *Wall Street Journal* bestselling
author of *The Unspoken Rules*

"The great leadership expert John C. Maxwell said 'Leadership is influence, nothing more, nothing less.' All great leaders and successful people know that influence is the key to success. Brad Englert gives us an amazing guide with *Spheres of Influence* on how to develop the art of influence for every type of business relationship in our lives and building healthy business relationships as an outcome!"

—Mike Lyles, international keynote speaker, author, and Maxwell Leadership Certified speaker, coach, and trainer

SPHERES

of

INFLUENCE

HOW TO CREATE
& NURTURE AUTHENTIC
BUSINESS RELATIONSHIPS

SPHERES

of

INFLUENCE

BRAD ENGLERT

FAST
COMPANY
Press

Fast Company Press
New York, New York
www.fastcompanypress.com

This work is being published under the Fast Company Press imprint by an exclusive arrangement with *Fast Company*. *Fast Company* and the *Fast Company* logo are registered trademarks of Mansueto Ventures, LLC. The Fast Company Press logo is a wholly owned trademark of Mansueto Ventures, LLC.

Distributed by Greenleaf Book Group

For ordering information or special discounts for bulk purchases, please contact Greenleaf Book Group at PO Box 91869, Austin, TX 78709, 512.891.6100.

Design and composition by Greenleaf Book Group
Cover design by Greenleaf Book Group

Publisher's Cataloging-in-Publication data is available.

Print ISBN: 978-1-63908-074-8

eBook ISBN: 978-1-63908-075-5

To offset the number of trees consumed in the printing of our books, Greenleaf donates a portion of the proceeds from each printing to the Arbor Day Foundation. Greenleaf Book Group has replaced over 50,000 trees since 2007.

Printed in the United States of America on acid-free paper

24 25 26 27 28 29 30 31   10 9 8 7 6 5 4 3 2 1

First Edition

To Corliss, Eric, and Nathan

CONTENTS

PREFACE

THIS BOOK IS DESIGNED TO HELP PROFESSIONALS who see themselves as emerging leaders. My hope is that aspiring professionals will have a clear road map for how to develop the critical hard skill of creating and nurturing effective business relationships. You can develop authentic business relationship skills just like you can learn other hard skills such as computer programming if you adhere to the basic principles and practice. You do not need to be born with the ability to build authentic business relationships.

Your professional relationships span two spheres of influence. The internal sphere of influence focuses on those people you can have the most direct impact with: your boss, executive leaders, direct reports, and all your staff. The external sphere of influence includes business relationships where you have less direct impact: customers, peers and influencers, and strategic vendor partners. The chapters are designed to stand on their own but can be read sequentially.

Three principles described in this book apply to all business relationships: Understand their goals and aspirations, set and manage their expectations, and genuinely care about their success. The crunchy, real-world stories shared in this book are relevant to a diverse range of industries, organizations, and backgrounds.

My purpose here is to describe the ways to build a variety of authentic, mutually beneficial, trusting, and enduring business relationships spanning years and often decades. Mutually beneficial professional relationships should begin early in your career and grow over many years. All business relationships are built on trust. The litmus test of an authentic business relationship is whenever you reconnect you pick up right where you left off—there is no time gap.

We need to transcend traditional networking, which tends to be transactional, short-lived, and—in my experience—superficial. It is difficult to engage in meaningful conversations, create rapport, or build trust with traditional networking, especially if the participants go in with a "What's in it for me?" mindset. Networking events rarely lead to unexpected opportunities or long-term business relationships. In addition, you cannot rely on social media's likes, shares, and links to build meaningful professional relationships.

After graduate school, I was fortunate to join Arthur Andersen & Co.'s Management Information Consulting Division, which became Andersen Consulting and then became Accenture. Throughout the book, I will refer to all three organizations as "the firm." After Accenture, I served as the chief information officer at The University of Texas at Austin. My best advice at the university came from a wise and crusty 40-year member of the faculty I had worked with on a successful strategy project 12 years prior. He growled, "Get out of the office, and tell people you give a damn!"

My former bosses, direct reports, staff, customers, colleagues, peers and influencers, and strategic vendor partners have asked if their experiences, achievements, and issues would appear in this book. Absolutely, but I promise anonymity. All the names of the people have been changed to protect both the innocent and the guilty, and no companies on either my most favored vendor list or my most hated vendor list have been named.

Thanks to all of you for the joys and pain you have given me over the years.

PART 1

The
INTERNAL
SPHERE
of
INFLUENCE

Chapter 1

RELATIONSHIP WITH THE BOSS

ESTABLISHING AND BUILDING AN EFFECTIVE RELATIONSHIP WITH your boss is one of the most important hard skills in business. You need to consciously work with your supervisor in order to get the best results for them, your organization, and yourself. In my experience, your boss will appreciate you initiating a conversation regarding what is important to them and how you can help them be more successful. Some managers are good at communicating their expectations, but some are not. It is your job to seek to understand what your boss's expectations are. Managing the expectations of your supervisor avoids confusion on both sides and shows them that you are engaged and curious—both traits they look for in leaders. In order to help your boss be successful, you must genuinely care about their success. Demonstrate that you care by offering options to resolve problems, and by demonstrating grit and the will to succeed.

UNDERSTAND YOUR BOSS

It is your responsibility to understand the goals and aspirations of your boss. First, you need to clarify when you don't fully understand a directive. Then you need to determine your boss's goals and how you align with them. Finally, figure out what you have to offer—and offer it.

Just ask!

It is a simple step, but many of us do not take the time to ask. If you don't know or understand your manager's goals, you may focus on the wrong tasks and waste your valuable time. Simply ask: "What are your goals, priorities, and pressures?"

Many bosses have sales or project targets that increase every year. You need to understand those targets and how you can do your part to help your supervisor achieve or exceed those goals. One supervisor said that meeting these ever-growing sales targets was like "feeding a bulldog: It's always hungry and keeps getting bigger."

Your overarching goal is to not be on any list that would put your boss on a list; for example, uncollected fees, late time reports, and delinquent performance evaluations. Let's say you're an account manager. Your supervisor is probably evaluated on how timely fees are collected. Fees not collected are subject to additional interest charges if not billed on time. Ensuring that all of your accounts are well managed helps your supervisor be successful. In addition, time and expenses must be entered by the deadlines—no exceptions. Personnel evaluations that are your responsibility must all be completed on time. Independent quality assessments of your projects must be rated high. Compliance coursework must be completed on time. Everything you do—or don't do—reflects on your manager. This is all within your control.

One supervisor I worked with was not forthcoming. He prided himself on being a chess master, "thinking many steps ahead." He thought that keeping his moves to himself was a strength. This technique was actually a dirty trick used to disorient and destabilize others while he consolidated power. In *The 48 Laws of Power*, Robert Greene cites "law three: Conceal your intentions: Keep people off-balance and in the dark by never revealing the purpose behind your actions. If they have no clue what you are up to, they cannot prepare a defense. Guide them far enough down the wrong path, envelop them in smoke, and by the time they realize your intentions it will be too late."[1] If I and the boss's other direct reports had known where he was heading, we would have been better positioned to help him achieve his goals. He declined, which was frustrating for me and all of his direct reports. Don't be a boss who keeps your moves to yourself.

When you have to work for a bad manager, take note of their dysfunctional behaviors so you can avoid these toxic characteristics when you are a supervisor. Refer to Greene's *The 48 Laws of Power* to recognize the ploys being used against you. Once you recognize what you are up against, you will be in a better position to protect yourself. You also have to grin and bear it. If your boss has a big ego, try to get them to think your ideas are their ideas. If they won't listen to you, try to find others in the organization to support and advise you, especially if they are admired by your manager. If your boss is untruthful, there is not much you can do. By all means protect your direct reports and staff from your supervisor's dysfunctional behaviors.

You need to consciously work with your boss—if they let you—in order to get the best results for them, your organization, and yourself. In my experience, your boss will appreciate you initiating a conversation regarding what is important to them and how you can help them be more successful.

Determine how you align with your boss's goals

After you have a good understanding of your boss's goals, self-reflect on your strengths, weaknesses, and work style to determine how they can be aligned with your boss's strengths, weaknesses, and work style. Some supervisors make quick decisions, some cannot make decisions when first asked, and some have difficulty making decisions at all. Without understanding your own strengths, weaknesses, and work style, you can't align them with someone else's. There are several tools to help you with self-assessment: CliftonStrengths Assessment by Don Clifton, the SOCIAL STYLE Model by TRACOM Group, and *I-Speak Your Language* by DBM Publishing.

Is your boss a lark who works early, or a night owl who comes in later and works late? I am a night owl, so when my manager was a night owl, we were naturally aligned. When I worked for a lark, I made sure to arrive to work early to stay aligned.

Some supervisors want to hear only the big picture, while others want to get into all the details. You need to adjust accordingly. Peter F. Drucker says in *Managing Oneself* that you need to know if your boss is "a reader or [a] listener."[2] A reader will want written proposals, and a listener will prefer hearing the proposals. You will frustrate a boss if you do not know which style they prefer.

I had a boss who could not make decisions when first asked. He always needed more space and time to think, and he felt cornered when first asked to make a decision. I learned to always begin a discussion with, "I'm not asking for a decision today; I just want your input." Then, in a second meeting, I would ask for a decision. I dubbed this approach the "Texas two-step," and it worked well for both of us. In addition, he was not a reader. He would be terse when using email but much more welcoming when discussing issues in person. So I made sure to discuss all sensitive issues in person.

One of my best managers at the firm would challenge me with field promotions. I wanted to be a leader, and she wanted to train future leaders, so our goals aligned perfectly. She would give me opportunities for stretch roles where I could act like a manager before I was a manager. Later in my career, she asked me to serve in executive roles while I was still a senior manager. The brilliance of this approach is that I could try new roles knowing that when I encountered challenges, there was no harm, no foul. Stretch roles were treated as lower-risk learning experiences. The added benefit of this approach was to build confidence in myself and my supervisor that I would be successful at the next level. You don't want to be promoted too early only to fail.

Offer your services

What do you enjoy and excel at? I was attracted to strategy work. Helping organizations understand where they are and articulate where they want to be in three to five years was fun and rewarding. Nearly all of the strategy projects I worked on resulted in follow-on engagements that grew the pie for my boss and myself. Because I enjoyed it and was good at it, I offered this skill to my manager.

I also enjoyed leading the development of client proposals. Writing a proposal is a grueling assignment, often with a short deadline. Proposal development is costly and can easily degenerate into a death march. However, with a well-thought-out plan, it is possible to create a high-quality proposal on time and within budget. Successful proposals articulate that we truly understand the client's request, convey fresh ideas and approaches, and propose a talented team to solve their business problems in a cost-effective way.

Once, I saw a public notice that a large public entity was going to award strategy work to a competitor "unless a better proposal was received." I suggested to my manager that we submit a better proposal and offered my services. We were happily surprised when we were selected to do the strategy work, which led to three lucrative follow-on projects.

Understanding what I enjoyed and excelled at led to volunteering to lead strategy work and creating successful proposals. This resulted in more work for my company, which helped my supervisor—and me—achieve our ever-increasing sales targets. This was the best approach for me. However, you need to determine which of your strengths can help your boss be most successful.

It is your responsibility to ask your manager what their goals and aspirations are, and after self-reflection, to offer how you can help achieve those goals. Do not be on any list that would put your supervisor on a list. And remember, when you become the boss, to proactively share your goals and aspirations with your direct reports. Hey, they are not mind readers.

MANAGE EXPECTATIONS

Some managers are good at communicating their expectations, but some are not. It is your job to seek to understand what your boss's expectations are. The following steps will help you manage the expectations of your boss.

Say "Whoa!"

One of my bosses had a type A personality: She worked fast, liked control, was highly competitive, and had a strong desire to succeed. Nine times out of ten, when you were called to her office, you were anticipating that something was wrong, and you steeled yourself for some verbal tough love.

Naomi Karten's book *Managing Expectations: Working with People Who Want More, Better, Faster, Sooner, NOW!* offers pragmatic advice on how to manage expectations and dramatically improve your effectiveness. Karten holds a BA and an MA in psychology and has extensive experience in technical, customer support, and management positions. After reading her book, I was able to better set expectations and maintain a greater balance between my professional and personal life. For example, when appropriate, say "whoa" to your supervisor.[3] Saying no is usually not well-received, especially with those managers with type A personalities. Saying "whoa," however, creates some time and space to truly understand what the boss is asking you to do. Slow the conversation down, and make sure you understand what is being asked.

The day after reading Karten's book, my type A boss called me at five p.m. with what, at first, appeared to be an urgent request. I was actually trying to leave the office on time for once to meet my wife for dinner. She sputtered, "I need a white paper—A WHITE PAPER on function point analysis! Do you know what that is?"

After taking a deep breath, I literally said, "Whoa!" and asked, "When do you need this?"

She abruptly stopped and paused to check her calendar: "Um, I need it in two weeks. Yes, I meet with the client again in two weeks."

I was thinking she needed it the next day. Taking the time to clarify expectations gave us both some much-needed mental space and reduced the stress of an imaginary tight deadline.

Then I asked, "How many pages should this white paper be?"

"Three to five," she replied.

I was thinking 10 pages, so again, saying "whoa" made the request clearer.

"Do you have an example of what you are looking for?"

"Yes. Ask Daniel for a copy of a white paper on XYZ corporation that I wrote ten years ago."

I smiled and left the office on time knowing that I would be able to enlist my staff to help the next morning. We had plenty of time to conduct the research and draft the white paper for the boss's review well before the client meeting.

Before I learned how to manage my supervisor's expectations

by saying "whoa," I would have cancelled dinner with my wife, frustrating her and upsetting me, worked all night to develop a 10-page white paper, and the next day gotten yelled at for not meeting my boss's expectations. That's a lose–lose–lose proposition all the way around.

Instead, with all that information, my supervisor's request was more manageable, I had a model to follow, and the deadline was further out than I had imagined. I never would have known if I hadn't had the courage to say "whoa." This was a turning point in the relationship with my supervisor, which gave me insight into how I needed to be clear on setting expectations and deadlines when I became the boss.

Set expectations from the outset

It is critical to set expectations from the outset with a new manager. It avoids confusion on both sides and shows them that you are engaged and curious—both traits they look for in leaders.

One of my new supervisors had a direct report peer of mine, Frank, who was the boss's close and trusted confidant. They had worked together for 13 years, and I was new. Early on, my boss would clearly seek and often take advice from Frank on many aspects of my department: budget, personnel, and policies. Frank would give advice that he didn't have the expertise to give, and he even started to create conflict where there wasn't any.

Some of my boss's emails giving me orders were clearly ghostwritten by Frank. Emails actually written by my supervisor, often via his mobile phone, were short, all caps, with no subject line. Frank's ghostly emails were confusing clouds of words, sent by my supervisor minutes after the two of them had met.

(I would check Frank's calendar to confirm the timing.) One email from my manager actually said, "I am not sending you this note because someone has whispered this in my ear." This dysfunctional work dynamic was both hilarious and sad. I always wondered if I would have an opportunity to ghostwrite email orders from the boss to Frank, but that never happened.

In a one-on-one meeting with my boss, I drew on a sheet of paper three heads with headsets all connected with coiled wires. Below the first head, I wrote, "offensive coordinator." Below the middle head, I wrote, "head coach." And below the third head, I wrote, "defensive coordinator." Then I said, "You are the head coach. Frank is your long-time, trusted offensive coordinator, and I am the new defensive coordinator. Your job is to hold Frank accountable for the offense (his department) and to hold me accountable for the defense (my department). When I get Frank's orders through your headset, you no longer need me. So, I expect that from now on you will hold Frank accountable for his domain and me accountable for my domain." My supervisor understood and thanked me for the "open and honest feedback." I set expectations for what I was comfortable with, and my boss embraced the feedback.

You are responsible for setting clear expectations with your supervisor from the outset, especially if you find yourself in a dysfunctional relationship. You must stand up for yourself in a professional and respectful way.

Be honest if you cannot help

In any relationship, sometimes you do need to say no. If you do not have the experience or skills to take on a role, you need to be honest. Say you cannot help, and offer recommendations on who would be a better fit for the opportunity. Recognizing the talents of others is part of becoming a leader, and a good manager will appreciate your honesty and your willingness to promote the best outcome for the team rather than yourself.

If you have prior family commitments, you owe it to your family and yourself to use your words and say no. As I mentioned earlier, I'm embarrassed to say that I cancelled several of my family vacations over the years due to my poor planning and expectation setting. Thanks to Naomi Karten, I learned the skill of how to take vacations and fulfill family commitments. Communicating early and often with your boss about family obligations gives everyone plenty of time to make backup plans. Reminding your supervisor each month leading up to the vacation helps everyone avoid surprises. I still feel guilty about asking one of my direct reports to cancel a vacation—which I did one time in 30 years. That was a mistake and was the direct consequence of me failing to think ahead.

Whether it's a family commitment or a mismatch of skills, a good manager will appreciate your honest admission that you're not a good fit for a project. Don't just say yes to everything; think about it, and make sure you can do a great job.

Be accountable and hold your boss accountable

You are responsible for meeting the expectations of your supervisor, as well as holding them accountable for providing the support and resources you need to be successful. This is easier said than done. If you are not provided the resources necessary to fulfill your organization's obligations, then you may fail at a project or goal. You are responsible for clearly communicating to the boss which obligations will no longer be met due to resource constraints they imposed. Be sure to communicate early to give your supervisor enough time to respond.

One time, my supervisor delayed the approval of the funding for the annual maintenance of some mission-critical assets. I wrote an email to her documenting that her decision to not fund this maintenance would put the enterprise at great risk and in default of state law. She then approved the funding. It's possible that she didn't see the consequences of her inaction, and holding her accountable helped both of us—and the enterprise—meet our responsibilities and goals.

Transparency

No one likes to be surprised, so err on the side of overcommunicating. Meet on a consistent basis to build trust and foster transparency. As issues arise, be sure to escalate when necessary. It is far better to seek your manager's advice to proactively address issues than to blindside them later. As Robert Vlasic, who headed the family-owned company of Vlasic pickles, often said, "Give me good news fast and bad news faster."[4]

Manage expectations with your supervisor by seeking to understand what is being asked, setting expectations from the outset, being honest about whether you can or cannot help, and fostering mutual accountability and transparency. Each of these mutual skills will reinforce your relationship, and they'll help you both ensure success.

GENUINELY CARE ABOUT THE SUCCESS OF YOUR BOSS

It is important for you to help your boss be successful—that is part of your own success. By exceeding expectations, you not only make yourself look good but make them look good as well. In order to do that, you must genuinely care about their success. You and your supervisor plus others who report to her are a team. You need to support your boss and others on the management team to achieve the best results for the organization.

Offer options to resolve problems

When presenting your manager with a problem, be prepared with several options to resolve the problem. You are closest to an issue and are best positioned to think through alternative approaches. Be patient and take the time to determine the root causes of the problem. Discussing the pros and cons of options to resolve problems with your supervisor is a great way to create collaborative solutions. If you arrive empty-handed, the boss will feel like she has to do all the thinking and will wonder why you are working for her. If you instead come prepared with solution options, you'll prove your value. You may not have the perfect answer, but your manager will appreciate that you didn't leave all the thinking to her or corner her into the role of being a rescuer.

Enlist support

There is no shame in asking your manager for help. In fact, it is quite the opposite. Not asking for help when you need it often leads to disaster. Sometimes, you need help to reign in the scope of a project. Other times, you may need more time to complete an initiative with quality. Often, more resources are required. In my experience, most supervisors welcome this discussion. However, some are not open to providing the requested support. In that case, you still need to explain why the support is needed and the consequences of not providing it.

One organization's leader had this mantra: "There's no money!" So, his direct reports and their teams stopped asking for the resources necessary to support the enterprise. Over time, needed equipment replacement was neglected, maintenance was out of support, and in some cases, the work environment was unsafe. Staff training was cut, and the entire organization's morale plummeted, resulting in poor service delivery. In reality, there were ample funds, but the egocentric leader set all the priorities. Instead of being cowed, his direct reports should have enlisted the boss's support to change the priorities and explain the consequences and risks of not doing so. Not replacing equipment at the end of its life or maintaining it led to unpredictable, high-profile outages that put the entire enterprise at risk. The boss's priorities finally shifted in order to prevent further embarrassing and costly unplanned outages, but the fiascos could have been entirely avoided if the team had stepped up and intervened earlier.

One team leader had the courage to let her manager know that she had a number of concerns. In a heartbreaking email to the boss, she said, "I am personally dissatisfied with the quantity and quality of my work over the past nine months. I don't think that I am doing the job you desire nor the department deserves. I still feel some pushback from my direct reports. It feels like they want to hear from you directly, rather than accept my direction and decisions. Many times, I have led them to this perspective by my not being sure what direction you want to go, and hence postponing a decision until we have spoken. This is not healthy for me or for the department. It is not clear to me what things I am responsible for and have the freedom to act on, nor what things you have taken responsibility for. I need clearer direction about how you intend for you and me to interrelate. What does it mean when you do not respond to my emails? I hope we can talk about this sometime soon."

The manager replied, "First, thank you very much for laying out your concerns. Second, your deep knowledge of the enterprise and our department, steady hand, and aggressive follow-through are making a substantial difference. Third, I respect you too much to discount your concerns. Let's find time to engage on this as soon as possible."

Because the executive had the courage to ask her manager for help, they were able to develop an authentic and trusting working relationship over a number of years.

Sometimes you have to ask the boss more than once, but this does not always work. One time, I was discussing with Ron, my supervisor, the idea of teaming with another company on a bid for a long-standing client of the firm. The other company would bring point expertise to our team that would serve the client well. Unfortunately, there were some building tensions between that company and our firm. Ron's response was, "Brad, I admire your courage to ask me again." Long pause. "But let me be crystal frigging clear: No!!!" We never teamed with the other company, and our client lost out. But I did my part to advocate for what I thought was best and never regretted it. Even more, my boss truly appreciated my fighting for the customer.

Try to enlist support from the manager when needed. Make the case for changing scope, timelines, or resources. Advocate for why you need their help, and explain the consequences of not obtaining the requested support. But be prepared to hear yes or no.

Demonstrate grit and the professional will to succeed

Why do some people have extraordinary success and others do not? What makes the difference—aptitude and innate ability or dedication to goals and strenuous effort? In her book *Grit: The Power of Passion and Perseverance*, Angela Duckworth, a psychology professor at the University of Pennsylvania, posits that it is not just talent but grit, a combination of passion and perseverance in pursuit of long-term goals, that matters most in achieving success.[5]

As a seventh-grade math teacher in a New York public school, Duckworth wondered why her most capable students did not always receive the best grades. She observed that those who got the best grades often chose to invest more time and effort in their work. Over the years, she studied entering West Point cadets, spelling bee champions, Ivy League undergraduates who had high SAT scores, and teachers working in some of the nation's most challenging schools, and she interviewed dozens of high achievers from chief executive officers to professional cartoonists and coaches. She repeatedly found that grit predicts success better than innate ability.

While grit is defined by tireless effort, it is demonstrated by consistency over time. Perseverance and endurance are what make the grittiest people—those who have long-term goals and the ability to work steadily and unfailingly to achieve them. Demonstrate your true grit to your boss. When the going gets tough—and it will—the ability to endure is one of the best and most important ways to contribute to the greater good.

Of course, you have to have talent as well. I do not sing well, so a career for me in opera is not an option. At the firm, there is a can-do mindset and a willingness to commit the resources to deliver on what was promised. This culture fosters tenacious support for customers and employees.

A manager once said to me, "You are tireless. You never quit! You are willing to work whatever hours and do whatever is required for the success of our clients and the firm. However, you need to do a better job balancing the firm's requirements with those of yourself and your family. You need to become a better role model for your direct reports and staff."

Demonstrate true grit, a can-do mindset, and the professional will to succeed to demonstrate that you genuinely care about the success of your manager, but don't overdo it.

Apologize for your mistakes

We all make mistakes. Honestly discussing with your manager what happened and what you will do differently in the future to avoid a reoccurrence is vitally important. It shows that you understand the problem and have thought through options and improvements. These are valuable skills. The good news is that the art of apology can be learned. Gary Chapman and Jennifer Thomas have discovered the following five fundamental aspects of an apology in their book *The Five Languages of Apology: How to Experience Healing in All Your Relationships*:

- Expressing regret—"I am sorry."

- Accepting responsibility—"I was wrong."

- Making restitution—"What can I do to make it right?"

- Genuinely repenting—"I'll try not to do that again."

- Requesting forgiveness—"Will you please forgive me?"[6]

Here is a message from my supervisor indicating that I screwed up: "Your proposal is fundamentally different from the direction I outlined yesterday. If you have concerns with this approach, we should discuss them before an alternative proposal is suggested to others."

I replied, "Sorry, I missed the mark. I was wrong. No concerns. Looking forward to discussing a course correction tomorrow."

Have the courage to apologize, and it will pay off in learning and growth. But apologize in moderation. Over-the-top apologies beyond what is needed may be perceived as weakness.

Be sensitive to chemistry, timing, and leadership voids

Understanding a new supervisor's goals and expectations is critical, just like with the old boss. Be open to their coaching, and adapt to their work style. At times, you will encounter someone who does not start from a foundation of trust. Or they may be part of a new executive leadership team with new priorities. And if the chemistry is not right, there is not much you can do, especially if they think you are not their person.

For example, a new boss questioned a strategic initiative approved by the prior executive leadership team. She speculated, "There was not a case made for change."

I replied, "Well, we actually created a master plan for this initiative that was unanimously endorsed by the prior executive leadership team. The first chapter of this master plan was entitled 'A Case for Change.'"

The new boss basically implied that if it happened before she arrived, it didn't exist. She also didn't appreciate being corrected, so I knew at that moment the chemistry was not right and it was time for me to move on, which I did soon after.

Serving an interim boss can also be challenging. Often, the interim boss is in the running for the permanent position and unlikely to rock the boat with their own boss. Decision-making can be slow or nonexistent. One of my interim bosses would not hold her other direct reports, my peer colleagues, responsible for actively participating in a major transformation project. In this leadership void, they were enabled to feign ignorance and play the victim.

She was a Jedi master at Greene's law four: "Always say less than necessary. Powerful people impress and intimidate more by saying less. The more you say, the more likely you are to say something foolish."[7] She would sit in every meeting and not say a word while the enterprise burned. When the new permanent boss arrived, all his direct reports were expected to own their share of the transformation initiative, which became a key to future success.

One smart and talented peer colleague began working in a new role for the CEO, who was not known for having warm interpersonal skills. There was no chemistry between the two. My colleague lamented to me that she felt like a dog in a new home: "Am I allowed to jump on the couch?" She just did not know what she was expected to do and left the enterprise after a year of frustration.

There may be a time in your career when you report to two supervisors. Reporting to multiple bosses can be challenging because you are balancing two sets of expectations. Be sure your job description and performance goals clearly document these expectations and the amount of time you devote to each manager's priorities. Sometimes having two supervisors is like having no leader, so you need to speak up when you need clear direction.

Thankfully, I had only one bad boss at the firm. He wanted me to focus solely on meeting my sales targets. Nothing else mattered to him. My skills and experience were more suited for delivering complex implementation engagements than sales. Over the years, the firm's senior leadership often asked me to help fix large, troubled projects. But my new boss directed me to focus only on sales. He did not try to take advantage of my strengths by connecting me to larger implementation roles like my prior manager did. Also, one of my responsibilities assigned by my prior manager was to coordinate the higher education practice in the US.

The new manager told me "to fake it" in this coordination role. Faking it is not my style. Fortunately, soon after he tried to fire me, the senior management team assigned me to a new role that better suited my skills and which delivered much more value for the firm. Fortunately, the senior management team also took swift action after the pattern of the bad boss's toxic behavior was finally discovered.

When your supervisor changes, be sensitive to the chemistry, timing, and leadership voids. Understand the new supervisor's goals and expectations. Be open to coaching and adapt to their work style.

Establishing and building an effective relationship with your supervisor is your responsibility and one of the most important hard skills in business. You need to consciously work with your boss in order to get the best results for them, your organization, and yourself. In my experience, your boss will appreciate you initiating a conversation regarding what is important to them and how you can help them be more successful.

KEY TAKEAWAYS

- Understand your boss's goals and aspirations.

- Set and manage their expectations.

- Genuinely care about your supervisor's success.

Chapter 2

RELATIONSHIPS WITH EXECUTIVE LEADERS

AT VARIOUS POINTS IN YOUR CAREER, YOU will likely be asked to work with executive leaders. Prepare for these opportunities by learning more about the enterprise. Executive leaders are the group of people with the most important positions in the enterprise: founders, presidents, senior vice presidents, vice presidents, chief executive officers, chief financial officers, chief marketing officers, chief operating officers, chief information officers, members of the board of directors—and in the public sector—appointed and elected officials. Fostering these relationships can accelerate your own career advancement, and you will differentiate yourself from other employees by understanding the purpose of the organization and offering to help.

First, you need to understand the organization's strategy and goals. Strategy is about positioning the organization relative to its competitors. Understanding strategy helps you work in concert with the organization's leadership. Aligning your own goals and actions with the organization's strategy, culture, and goals will also add value that can accelerate your career advancement.

Second, you must set and manage expectations. Everyone has expectations, and those expectations are difficult to control. You can dramatically improve your effectiveness by understanding what is being asked, agreeing on the scope of a proposed solution at the beginning, and being honest about whether you can help. It is much easier to make corrections to expectations at the start and to realign them along the way than it is to discover a catastrophic and possibly irreparable mismatch later.

Third, as with your boss, you must genuinely care about the success of your executive leaders. These are three crucial aspects of building effective relationships with your leadership team.

UNDERSTANDING THE ORGANIZATION

The best way to align yourself with executive leadership is to understand the organization's strategy and culture. Understanding your organization's strategy and culture helps you better fit into the organization and work with leadership. The steps to understanding the organization are similar to how you understand your boss.

Zoom out from the narrow perspective of your current role to better understand the wider purpose of the enterprise. Review the organization's website and annual reports to better learn about the strategy, mission, vision, values, goals, and culture. Align your actions and goals to work in concert with what you learn.

Determine how you align with those goals. Step back and ask how you can support the achievement of the organization's goals. What can you offer to attain those goals? Ask yourself, "What capabilities can I bring to the table? What solutions can I offer?" How would you help define the organization's strategy, if none exists? You can prove your value by offering to help create a strategy.

Learn about your enterprise

In the private sector, you can find strategies in the company's annual report and quarterly earnings statements. Company websites typically convey strategies, mission statements, visions, goals, values, and culture. Strategies are planned courses of action to differentiate a company. Mission statements are simple and concise declarations of the purpose of an organization. Visions describe what a company is building toward in the future. Goals are measurable objectives that organizations set in order to improve performance. Values are the internal beliefs and principles that drive the business. Culture is the set of attitudes, practices, customs, and norms that define an organization for employees and externally as an aspect of its public image. All these are crucial pieces of the puzzle that make up any organization.

In the public sector, agency websites also convey strategies, mission, vision, goals, values, and culture of an organization. Reviewing promulgating legislation related to an agency is a good place to start to understand that organization's purpose and goals. Strategy documents are public information and are typically readily available online.

Once you understand an organization's strategy, culture, and goals, you are better positioned to work with executive leaders. You'll understand how your organization stands relative to its competitors. Your understanding will help you work in concert with the organization's leadership when the time comes and with your fellow employees to reach a mutual overarching goal. Demonstrating that you understand the organization's culture through your interactions with your colleagues will ensure your fit with the organization and showcase your value for the leadership.

Determine how you align with those goals

Step back and ask how you can support the achievement of the goals you've discovered for your enterprise. Ask yourself what ideas, skills, knowledge, and abilities you can bring to the table.

Demonstrate a passionate desire to learn about the business, and try to exceed executive leadership's expectations when you have the opportunity to work with them. Ask good questions and actively listen. Seek to understand, and solve problems with initiative, integrity, empathy, and competence. Find solutions to problems and ask for support when you need it. This is what makes you a memorable employee: someone who learns, grows, and eventually leads.

At times, you will not be able to align with executive leaders. One time, my firm proposed to conduct a performance review of a large state agency. In the oral presentation of our proposal, an agency executive leader asked, "Will you be open, honest, and independent during the review?" We answered, "Yes, of course!" We were not selected. Later via an open records request, we obtained the evaluation scores. Our firm scored highest in the proposed approach and lowest in cost. The selected firm scored fifth out of seven proposals. When that firm was asked whether they would be open, honest, and independent during their review, we believe that they answered the question this way, "We will work with you to be sure you are happy with the end result." Thank goodness we were not selected. The executive leaders in this story did not want honesty, and that was a clear sign that it was better for us not to work for them. You will be happier when you align with your leaders. It reduces conflict and ensures that both you and the leadership will value your work with them.

The best way to build effective business relationships with executive leadership is to understand the organization's purpose, strategy, goals, and problems. Take the initiative to help solve problems. If executive leaders are receptive to your offer of assistance, look for patterns, recommend tailored solutions, and tactfully take a stand when necessary.

What can you offer toward those goals?

Once I was asked a great question from a business school student: "What exactly do consultants do?" I replied, "We find solutions to problems. No one ever calls for help when they have no problems, lots of time, and plenty of money. Usually, there are lots of problems, no time, and little money."

Unfortunately, some executive leaders do not listen to their employees. Then they bring in external consultants who do listen; that's me. The old saying is "a consultant takes your watch off to tell you the time." Well, that's somewhat true, and it's worth every penny if a leader refuses to look at their wrist.

When I presented an employee's idea for improving a bank's performance in a trust division, the president publicly chastised me for "stealing that idea from Mike."

I countered, "Yes, Mike raised this smart idea five years ago, and no one listened. You should have listened to him. Now is the perfect time to act, and we should give Mike all the credit."

After you've asked yourself what capabilities you can bring to the table and what options you can offer, you should then bring those alternative solutions to your executive leaders. High-performing organizations listen to their employees and encourage collaborative problem solving. This tells you about the culture of the organization. If an executive leader sees asking for help to address areas of concern as a sign of weakness, you will never be heard and appreciated for your contribution. In this situation, seek support for your ideas from other executive leaders.

How would you help define an organization's strategy, if none exists?

It is shocking how many organizations do not have a strategy or have not updated a strategy developed many years ago by a prior executive leadership team. If your organization does not have a strategy, offer to help create one. Strategy is about positioning the organization relative to its competitors. Graham Kenny's article "Strategic Planning Should Be a Strategic Exercise" emphasizes that "all organizations have competitors, for staff, for funds, for resources."[1]

The process to develop a strategy is straightforward: Gather internal and external data, create a vision and define objectives, identify strategic initiatives, prioritize, estimate costs, and build an implementation plan. Gather data through one-on-one interviews, focus groups of major constituents, online surveys, and peer benchmarking. As you gather data on the organization, document its physical assets and assess the staff's capabilities. Identify the gaps between the vision/objectives and assets/capabilities in order to define strategic initiatives to address the gaps. Also, be sure to understand cultural norms so the strategic initiatives are informed by culture. The three-to-five-year implementation plan should be supported with cost estimates for all the strategic initiatives and overall program management. You never know at the beginning of a strategic planning process what strategic initiatives or priorities will emerge, but like cream rising to the top of a milk bottle, they always reveal themselves.

Kenny advises, "Don't think of your strategic plan as fixed . . . *Strategy* originates from the Greek *strategos*, which means a general in command of an army. Military chiefs don't envisage that their plan of attack will remain static after contact with the enemy. Nor should you."[2] Any enterprise should update its strategic priorities and realign its resources on an annual basis.

Here are a few examples of this approach in action.

Two of the highest strategic priorities for a major university system were to expand a statewide high-speed data network and to establish a digital library to support all 13 health and academic institutions. The governing board invested to double the capacity of the statewide high-speed network. And a digital library was funded and built that has effectively served 240,000 students and

100,000 healthcare professionals, researchers, faculty, and support staff since 1998.

A human services agency needed to know who and where their clients were. The highest-priority strategic initiative was to design and build an electronic medical records system for 22 inpatient and 50 outpatient facilities underpinned with an integrated client database. Eighteen months later, the new system came online. We held a contest to guess how many unduplicated clients the agency served. The winning guess—250,000 clients as predicted by the commissioner. One week after the electronic medical records system was live, a police officer found a disoriented woman wandering along a busy highway. In her pocket was a torn envelope with half of a last name visible. The police contacted the human services agency, who located her new electronic medical record and determined that the client had left a nearby inpatient mental health facility, and she was returned to the facility for care.

A large research university's highest-priority strategic initiative related to information technology (IT) was to establish IT governance. There were 11 committees charged with various types of IT decision-making. We referred to the 11 committees as the "constellation of IT governance." Some committees had gravitational influence (bosses on some, their staff on others), some were floating in space with no stated purpose or direction, and others were black holes where questions were sucked in years ago and answers never came out. No one knew who made the decisions or why. Everyone on campus was so frustrated with the current state that the proposed new governance structure was fully embraced. All key strategic, operational, and technical recommendations were made thereafter with input from faculty, students, and staff and endorsed by executive leadership.

One new chief executive officer transitioning to lead an enterprise with a $3 billion annual budget announced that a strategic planning process would be conducted. Unfortunately, this never happened. The enterprise was rudderless for five years.

You never know at the beginning what the strategic initiatives or the priorities will be, which is nerve-wracking. Have faith in the proven strategic planning process, engage the right constituents, and inform the strategy with your organization's cultural norms. The highest strategic initiatives and priorities always reveal themselves like cream rising to the top of a milk bottle.

In the article "Can You Say What Your Strategy Is?" David J. Collis and Michael G. Rukstad observe that many leaders don't know what their strategy is: "It's a dirty little secret. Most executives cannot articulate the objective, scope, and advantage of their business in a simple statement. If they can't, neither can anyone else."[3] You can prove your value by helping to create the strategy.

Understanding an organization's culture, strategy, and goals is the foundation for building effective business relationships with executive leaders.

EXPECTATIONS

Everyone has expectations. Sometimes the expectations of executive leaders seem unreasonable. And sometimes your expectations of them seem just as unreasonable from their point of view. Expectations are difficult to control and impossible to turn off. And mismatched expectations lead to grievous misunderstandings.

I finally learned how to effectively work with executive leaders by setting clear expectations using techniques in Naomi Karten's book *Managing Expectations*. This section touches on some of her simple and effective techniques you too can employ.

Understand what is being asked of you

When an executive leader asks you to help solve a problem, it is important to actively listen and help them describe their needs. You must take the time to gather the facts and understand the context of a situation before proposing how to develop options. Karten proposes you should say: "Please let me first seek to understand what is being asked so we can align our expectations."[4]

Set expectations from the outset

When you are beginning an initiative, document the scope, timing, staffing, and budget. A one-page summary of the high-level objectives, activities, duration, and level of effort can be used to secure agreement at the start of an initiative and to anchor back throughout the effort in order to communicate progress to your executive leaders. A project charter—a short document that describes the scope of the work and anticipated benefits in clear, concise wording for executives' review and approval—is a helpful tool to set those executives' expectations.

One of my most demanding clients—in a good way—was the chancellor of a major public university system who had a PhD in business. He retained the firm to develop a strategy and demanded, "I do not want a fluffy consultant's report!" In our kick-off meeting with him and his executive leadership team, we discussed the project charter which presented the project objectives; proposed an approach, timing, and budget; and offered a draft table of contents for the strategy. We discussed the content that we would create in each section and even estimated the number of pages for each one. The chancellor and his executive team only adjusted the number of pages in one section and agreed with the proposed objectives, approach, staffing, timing, budget, and structure for creating the strategy. We could then use this as a blueprint for the work and also to hold each other accountable to those agreements throughout the process.

Gaining executive leadership buy-in regarding the scope of the final product at the beginning of the engagement reflects Stephen R. Covey's second habit (begin with the end in mind) from *The 7 Habits of Highly Effective People*. Covey says, "To begin with the end in mind means to start with a clear understanding of your destination. It means to know where you're going so that you better understand where you are now so that the steps you take are always in the right direction."[5]

Throughout the project with the chancellor, we met once a month with both him and the executive leadership team to discuss the work to date and what work was upcoming to confirm that expectations were still aligned. At the end of the strategic planning project, we delivered what was promised, and the strategy was unanimously endorsed by the chancellor and the executive leadership team.

Another time, the firm was asked to lead a massive administrative reengineering program at a top public research university. The program was behind schedule and over budget. However, based on an independent consultant's review and assessment, we had all the elements for success. I was asked to lead the program restart, which would begin in October and take at least a year.

When I had lunch at the faculty club with the provost and the chief financial officer, I said, "This role is a wonderful opportunity, and I'm certain we will be successful. However, I promised my wife and two boys that we would take a three-week vacation in June to Australia, where I was an exchange student in high school. I cancelled the trip last year because of work obligations and missed my 25th class reunion. Now passports are in hand, plane tickets have been purchased, and I cannot cancel again or risk another disappointment at home." The CFO and provost said they understood and agreed.

By April the following year, the team had successfully achieved another major milestone, and the program was back on budget and on schedule. During the monthly status meeting in May with the president, the CFO, and the provost, I reported that the program was on track and going well, reminding the president that I would be out of the country in June and that Debbie, one of my direct reports, would be in charge.

The president's face blanched, and his hands started shaking. As I opened my mouth in slow motion to cancel my vacation, the CFO interrupted me and said, "Hold on, Brad. Mr. President, when Brad joined us, the provost and I agreed that he would be able to take this long-planned vacation. It is very important to him and his family. He says this is the best time to be away from the program, and we trust him. We should honor our commitment."

The president agreed, and Debbie did a great job. Nine years later, at dinner with the CFO and our spouses, we recounted that story. He shared, "The provost and I were scared to death while you were away!"

In order to meet the expectations of executive leaders, you need to agree on the objectives, scope, timing, staffing, and budget at the beginning of an initiative. Use your words to set expectations related to your work–life balance, as well as the project itself.

Be honest if you cannot help

You may be asked by executive leaders to help solve problems beyond your skills, knowledge, or abilities. Be honest. Taking on a role where you are not equipped or prepared can lead to frayed nerves, misunderstandings, and failed projects. When appropriate, recommend someone who you think would be a better fit.

One executive leadership team asked Dennis, a loyal, long-standing employee, to lead the implementation of a massive payroll system. Unfortunately, Dennis had no experience leading a payroll implementation project, and he should have declined the role. After significant delays and cost overruns, the multimillion-dollar payroll system was moved into production before it was ready. However, many errors surfaced, including someone receiving a $1 million paycheck that they were reluctant to return. The executive leadership team realized that they had asked too much of Dennis and then recruited an experienced payroll system implementation leader. The project went on to be successful. Dennis did not suffer any repercussions, because executive leadership realized that it had been unfair for them to expect someone with no experience implementing payroll systems to be successful.

After completing a strategy for a midsize retail liquor store company, the executive leaders asked me to stay on to help implement the highest-priority initiative: an easy-to-use e-commerce website and mobile app supporting in-store pickup and home delivery. Given I wanted to start writing this book, I promised to find someone with deep e-commerce experience to help them. They retained Viji, a brilliant woman who worked with me 15 years earlier, to lead this transformational project. Viji was truly an e-commerce expert. She had created the e-commerce capability for a global technology company and built a medical marijuana website for a Canadian start-up—controlled substance sales over the web. Viji quickly implemented the sleek new website and mobile app in 40 stores. Then the pandemic hit. She worked with her team day and night to add the remaining 60 stores. This new sales channel was delivered just in time to serve evolving customer expectations, and it's fun for me to frequently take advantage of this new capability.

Be honest and open from the start. Don't just take a position because it's offered; make sure you can commit to the work and are a good fit—or are able to *become* a good fit by developing into it. If not, recommend someone better who can help.

Mutual accountability

You also need executive leaders to do what they are supposed to do. There are times when you need a decision to be made, but some leaders are uncomfortable with making decisions. You'll need to—carefully—help them realize their responsibility. The best executive leaders hold others accountable for success but are also accountable themselves.

During that university reengineering program, the provost, CFO, and president were visibly supportive from beginning to end. They explained to the multiple campus constituencies why the university was embarking on the implementation of multiyear administrative improvements and set expectations regarding anticipated benefits—and challenges—from the extensive changes ahead. They reviewed and approved our plans, timelines, staffing, and budgets. They provided strategic policy direction, and the provost and CFO cochaired the program's steering committee, composed of influential deans and administrative staff leaders. When a board member challenged the president and asked for another consultant to review the program's plans and estimates, the president shot back, "If you want to hire another consultant, you will have to hire another president." The board member demurred and said, "That is not what we are here to discuss."

When the steering committee met to decide whether to go live, someone said that they were nervous. The provost asked why. Their reply was, "I just am." The provost smiled and said, "Some level of anxiety is healthy. It keeps us all focused."

These executives provided air cover for the program. For example, the provost and CFO messaged the organization that the new payroll system "was targeted to go live on October 1." They added, "If we are not ready, then we will fall back to the Thanksgiving holiday." We tracked 30 go-live criteria. As we neared October 1, 16 indicators were green (*Go!*), 14 were yellow (*Caution!*), and there were no red indicators (*Showstoppers!*). However, the 14 yellow issues could not be resolved by October 1. Emotions were running high, since the combination of these 14 open yellow items introduced a high level of risk.

So the steering committee had the courage to delay the go-live date. This news was well received by the organization, because the senior executives had consistently communicated that any delay if we were not ready would be prudent and not be deemed a failure. In fact, we were able to resolve all 14 issues within two weeks, and we found a new go-live date in mid-October; no one wanted to work during the Thanksgiving holiday.

The resulting launch proved to be a nonevent. Both the provost and the CFO said afterward that this prudent decision to wait until we were ready demonstrated the maturity of the university.

In a similar program at another multibillion-dollar company, leadership change derailed accountability. After a new chief executive officer was hired, all the senior executive leaders left. The prior CEO and senior leadership team had unanimously approved the plan to replace the 30-year-old administrative processes and systems. But for more than a year and a half, interim executives were in place. The interim executives provided little leadership or accountability for themselves or their direct reports. Business owners who reported to the interim CFO feigned ignorance and played the victim, and the interim CFO did not hold anyone accountable. Moreover, the new CEO had no interest in this major program and, for more than a year, refused to even communicate the importance of this generational change to multiple constituencies, which led to significant delays and cost overruns.

Executive leaders are essential for setting and managing expectations for an organization, especially in times of massive change. If they are not willing to support the change program, additional costs, delays, and failures result. In the early stages of your career, you may not yet feel comfortable discussing with your supervisor when you experience a mismatch with the leadership. However, raising the issue shows your supervisor that not only are you paying attention but also care about the organization. Speak to your manager about mismatched expectations and discuss how you both can help gain the necessary executive leadership support.

Candor

Open and honest communication is a two-way street. Executive leaders need to define the direction ahead, explain how decisions are made, and establish a collaborative environment.

Just as the provost and CFO explained to their campus constituents why the university was embarking on the multiyear administrative improvement program, they also did not sugarcoat the disruption ahead: "Course corrections will be needed, and mistakes will need to be corrected. We ask for your patience and encourage your feedback. We stand ready to make the necessary adjustments in the years ahead."

The opposite example was an executive leader who said, "My door is always open" but bristled at any honest input. This executive actually had a "beat the messenger" disposition. People in the organization realized their honest feedback was not truly wanted, so they stopped giving it.

In my first meeting with the CFO of another large university system where the firm would be helping to implement new administrative systems, she challenged me by saying, "How can you waltz in here and know what is going on?"

My response was, "I have seen this movie before."

Pointing to a stack of reports on her desk, I asked, "How can you review those financial reports and know where the problems are?"

She laughed and said, "After 25 years, you know where to look."

"Me too," I said.

We had an excellent working relationship thereafter.

Candor should be reciprocal. When executive leaders seek and provide open and honest communication, trust and collaboration in an organization result.

GENUINELY CARE ABOUT THE SUCCESS OF EXECUTIVE LEADERSHIP

In order to demonstrate your value and to ensure your own motivation to contribute, you must be authentic and genuinely care about the success of your executive leaders. The steps to get there are similar to those for your boss.

Show up and listen

Never bring problems to executive leaders without first thinking through options to resolve them. As a partner with the firm, I was coached by one of my managers to meet with the CEO of my client's organization throughout the engagement. Once a month, like clockwork, I met the CEO to discuss how things were going. We both assigned the best and brightest employees to do the work, and for the first nine months, there were no issues. Over time, trust and goodwill were established between us.

Unfortunately, in the tenth month, I realized that the project team needed our help to successfully get us across the finish line, so I went to the CEO to discuss options. We both realized that we needed to increase our resources. Without hesitation, the CEO spun around from his desk, picked up the phone, called his project leader, and said, "Whatever additional resources you need, Lisa, you got 'em." We had a successful result. If I had waited until there was a major issue to first seek help from the CEO, I would have been viewed as the person only bringing problems. Building trust over time when there are no problems will help you become the person with solution options when problems do arise.

Stephen R. Covey observed in *The 7 Habits of Highly Effective People*, "Building and repairing relationships are long-term investments."[6] He created the metaphor of an emotional bank account that describes the amount of trust that has been built up in a relationship. Just like a financial bank account, you make deposits and build up a reserve in order to make withdrawals when needed. You make deposits by demonstrating "courtesy, kindness, honesty, and keeping commitments."[7] Covey suggested six major deposits that build an emotional bank account: "understanding the individual, attending to little things, keeping commitments, clarifying expectations, showing personal integrity, and apologizing sincerely when you make a withdrawal."[8] Create and nurture effective business relationships by understanding people "deeply as individuals, the way you would want to be understood, and then to treat them in terms of that understanding."[9]

Once, I received a thank-you gift from an executive leader. It was a hand-thrown pottery jar with "Solutions" carved on the side. She appreciated that I always brought options to resolve the problems we encountered.

Enlist support

Have the courage to ask your executive leaders for help. When I was serving as an acting chief information officer to create an information technology strategy for a large health sciences center, we established a steering committee composed of senior faculty and researchers from the School of Medicine, the School of Nursing, the School of Dentistry, the Graduate School of Biomedical Sciences, and the School of Health Professions. Unfortunately, the world-class researcher representing the School of Medicine did not show up for the first three steering committee meetings.

In my monthly status meeting with the president, I asked for her help, given the importance of having the medical school participate in the development of the strategy. She said, "Go ask the good doctor to participate, and if he still doesn't, I'll gently persuade him."

In my follow-up meeting with the researcher, his first comment was, "You are the first person from central IT to ever meet with me." I explained the importance of him participating to represent the School of Medicine, and he never missed another steering committee meeting. He became an outstanding advocate during the development and implementation of the IT strategy. He also served as the chairperson of the search committee that recruited the permanent chief information officer.

After I was asked to take over a troubled project to replace a payroll system, some of the technical staff were unhappy. A rumor surfaced that someone might sabotage the computer equipment in retaliation. I asked the CFO if we should inform the police. She smiled and said that she did not think that the technical staff would jeopardize their own paychecks. She was right—thank goodness—but even an unlikely scenario prompted me to ask for help, and it could have headed off a problem.

Ask for help from executive leaders when you need to do so. Asking for help is a strength, not a weakness. It takes courage to enlist support, and the consequences of not doing so can be disastrous.

Apologize when you screw up

Things will go wrong. You and your people will make mistakes. How we deal with these inevitable situations is key.

When serving as an executive leader of a large research university, I had ample opportunities to apologize and was the recipient of emails at times critical of the services my department provided. An email from a member of the faculty whose daughter was starting college in the fall said that she received a letter on my organization's letterhead from the campus computer store offering discounts on laptops: "I went online to check the price differences and found they ranged in savings from $0 to $5 on a $1,000 laptop computer. In my mind, this advertisement is at least disingenuous if not fraudulent. I wanted to bring this to your attention."

Of course, I was not aware that the campus computer store had sent these letters to all incoming freshmen on my organization's letterhead. The store was managed by a third-party vendor under contract, and the content of the letter had been approved many years prior by my predecessor's predecessor. My apology email to the mother thanked her for bringing this unfortunate incident to my attention, took responsibility for the miscue, explained the new steps that would keep it from happening again, and asked for forgiveness.

The key was to follow up on that promise of the incident not happening again. I took action to ensure that the store did not continue this practice. Covey says, "Sincere apologies make deposits; repeated apologies interpreted as insincere make withdrawals."[10]

Mistakes will happen. Be ready to accept responsibility, and practice the art of apology.

Be sensitive to chemistry and timing

I have worked with two types of executive leaders: team players and imperious dictators. Team players are humble practitioners who seek the best ideas from others and strive to help everyone succeed. The imperious dictator is dismissive of others, believes they are the smartest person in the room, and thinks they have all the answers. Fortunately, most of the executive leaders I have served over the past 30 years have been team players. These leaders start from a position of trust and have confidence in you. One of my executive leaders jokingly said that he wanted to implant an imaginary chip that would zap me if I ever thought of leaving the enterprise.

His successor, however, was an imperious dictator who thought he had all the answers and did not trust me or his other direct reports. Meeting with him was like stepping on a garden rake. Thwack! I knew it was time for me to leave.

Be sensitive to the chemistry you have or don't have with executive leaders. Most are team players in my experience.

Genuinely caring about the success of your executive leaders better positions you for career success. Offer options to solve problems. If you are likely to need help implementing those solutions, don't hesitate to ask for support. Finally, remember to apologize when you or your people make mistakes, and be sensitive to chemistry and timing. These are all crucial aspects of building relationships with your leadership team.

Creating and nurturing effective business relationships with executive leaders is a critical skill and your responsibility. Be ready when the time comes to work with executive leaders. Fostering relationships with executives can accelerate your career advancement. You will differentiate yourself from other employees by understanding the purpose of the organization and offering to help.

KEY TAKEAWAYS

- Seek to understand your organization's strategy and goals.

- Set and manage expectations of your executive leaders.

- Genuinely care about the success of your executive leaders.

Chapter 3

RELATIONSHIPS WITH DIRECT REPORTS

EFFECTIVE RELATIONSHIPS WITH THOSE WHO REPORT TO you are critical for the success of the organization. You must start with the assumption that everyone reporting to you is working in good faith toward the same goals. You need to demonstrate a trusting, humble, and honest approach to doing business. As the boss, you need to be a mentor, coach, visionary, cheerleader, confidant, guide, sage, trusted partner, and perspective keeper. It also helps to have a sense of humor.

It is first crucial to articulate the organization's values, set expectations, and establish mutual accountability. Then you can focus on creating a safe work ecosystem. Finally, you need to let your team leaders know you care about their success and growth and the success of their teams. Happy employees lead to happy customers, and in the private sector, happy shareholders.

VALUES, EXPECTATIONS, AND MUTUAL ACCOUNTABILITY

Beginning a new leadership role in an organization is an opportune time to establish and articulate the values of the organization and to make sure your team leaders understand what is expected of them. Document your expectations and establish mutual accountability. Be open and honest with your team leads, provide timely feedback, and let them know this relationship is a two-way street. These are invaluable steps to being an effective boss, and your team leads will appreciate it. If you are well beyond the first 90 days in a supervisory role, just start now.

Articulate organizational values—together

Taking over an organization provides the unique opportunity to establish, confirm, or redefine the values of the organization. If the organization has established values, meet one-on-one with your team leads to confirm these values and seek input toward improvement. Learn how each team works to support internal and external customers. If the organization does not have a clear set of values, collaborate with the team leaders to create one.

Here is an example of a department's set of values created by my direct reports and me:

- Put family first.

- Deliver high-quality services.

- Foster customer partnerships.

- Establish understanding, trust, and accountability.

- Make data-driven, innovative, customer-focused decisions.

- Facilitate collaboration, cooperation, and communication.

These values were prominently displayed on the organization's website and reinforced to all staff via quarterly meetings and frequent communications. Orientation sessions for all new employees were scheduled every month so they could learn about these organizational values, ask questions, and meet the management team leaders.

Make sure direct reports understand what is expected of them

Set clear expectations and establish a safe and honest work environment. Trust your direct reports until they give you reason to doubt them. Give them the freedom to manage their teams, and seek their feedback to find opportunities for improvement.

When my direct reports had an issue, I expected and trusted them to seek a resolution. All of my direct reports received a copy of the classic *Harvard Business Review* article by William Oncken Jr. and Donald L. Wass, "Management Time: Who's Got the Monkey?" My expectation was that they would be responsible for solving their problems (i.e., monkeys) and that I would not accept any monkeys from them.[1] The goal was to establish a culture where they were empowered to seek the optimal solutions to problems. Over time, you must help your direct reports to develop the ability to solve problems on their own. And as the boss, you are responsible for establishing trusting relationships with your team leads and should expect them to likewise delegate decisions and trust and develop the people on their teams.

Document measurable expectations for your team leads in their job descriptions and performance goals. Establish a continuous dialogue to mentor and guide the members of your management team. Also, the annual performance review cycle provides a formal opportunity to assess the past year's performance and to establish team and personal growth goals for the coming year. You will be rewarded by having team leaders who clearly understand what is expected of them.

The relationship is a two-way street

Open and honest discussion must be the norm, and there needs to be mutual accountability. Meet one-on-one with your team leads each week to discuss challenges, and collaborate to develop optimal responses. Always meet in their offices—not yours—as a sign of respect and so you are visible to their team members.

One new team leader was concerned about a project that was scheduled to be completed by her predecessor "during the coming summer." She was nervous to ask me to extend the schedule, given that we had just started working together. Fortunately, she had the courage to ask and was extremely relieved when I said the schedule could be extended: "It has taken us 40 years to get to this point, so another few weeks or months is not material in the grand scheme of things."

Moving a date and producing an excellent result is far better than meeting a date with poor quality. It never pays to rush completion just to meet a date. If more resources are needed to meet a date, so be it. If more time is needed to deliver the expected quality and results, your team lead must be comfortable discussing the need to adjust the timeline with you and your customers. Team leads must take the time to continually communicate with you, their customers, and colleagues in order to deliver high-quality results on time and on budget. A team leader who cuts corners to meet promised deadlines—often with disastrous results—erodes trust. Encourage your direct reports to ask for help when they need more time or resources to produce an excellent result.

Another new team leader asked, "How am I doing?"

My reply was, "I could not be happier. You are doing great. We are all so thankful you decided to join our organization. Your experience and style are a perfect fit."

Do not wait until the annual performance review to give positive or constructive feedback. If fact, err on the side of giving immediate feedback. Normalize giving immediate feedback. Model it. People always want to know if they are meeting your expectations as the boss. They are not mind readers.

One week after the firm promoted me to partner, I was sitting around a table discussing a current project with three senior consultants. After I said something I soon realized was dumb, I stopped and asked them, "Did you all realize what I said was dumb?"

They smiled and nodded their heads up and down and said, "Yes."

Astonished, I replied, "Well from this point forward, and even though I am now a partner, I expect you all to speak up when I say stupid things. The firm is paying you for your brainpower!"

You need to give your direct reports opportunities to be great; however, you also need to act if they are not honest. I learned later in my career to act sooner than later in these situations. Six months into a new role leading a large organization, one of my team leaders was withholding critical budgetary information on a $32 million construction project. I assigned Maggie, an experienced project manager, to help this team leader organize the financial data. When I confronted him, he admitted to concealing the data from me. Worse, he was not a team player. His team would randomly make changes without notice, which would negatively impact the work of customers, my other team leads, and my peer colleagues in other departments. On multiple occasions, I directed him to act, and he did not follow through. I then asked him to tell me beforehand if he did not understand what I was asking him to do, but he never did. Finally, I said, "You need to tell me if you are not going to do what is asked, so I can get someone else to do it."

This was the first and only time I fired someone right before the winter holidays. Afterward, several startling gaffes emerged from his lack of oversight of the construction project and his team's operations. The replacement team leader was light years more capable and always a straight shooter.

Be open and honest with your team leads, and encourage two-way communication. Establishing values, setting expectations, and instituting mutual accountability can be achieved by articulating the values of the organization, making sure your direct reports understand what is expected of them, providing timely feedback, and letting them know this relationship is a two-way street. When encountering dishonesty, take swift action. These are the steps to become an effective leader, and your direct reports will appreciate it.

CREATE A SAFE WORK ECOSYSTEM

One of your responsibilities to the people reporting to you is to create a safe work ecosystem. The first 90 days leading an organization is a unique opportunity to build camaraderie with your team leads and to learn what is working and where to make improvements.

Carolyn O'Hara, in her article "What New Team Leaders Should Do First" for *Harvard Business Review*, observed: "Getting people to work together isn't easy, and unfortunately, many leaders skip over the basics of team building in a rush to start achieving goals. But your actions in the first few weeks and months can have a major impact on whether your team ultimately delivers results."[2]

In the international bestseller *The First 90 Days: Proven Strategies for Getting Up to Speed Faster and Smarter*, Michael D. Watkins offers proven approaches to avoid the common pitfalls as you transition into a new leadership role. He describes how to prepare to take charge, accelerate your learning, secure early wins, and achieve alignment with your strategy, structure, systems, skills, and culture. In addition, he emphasizes the importance of building the team you have inherited and how to change it.[3]

Start with the expectation that your direct reports are doing their best to achieve organizational goals and then showcase your values. For example, I was asked by my team leads, "How do you make decisions?" My reply was that my decisions are "data driven and customer focused." This is also the time to establish trust and honesty as key values.

Together, we set the weekly cadence of one-on-one meetings and a team leaders meeting. We agreed on the approach for written status reports—for example, once a week, one page, with issues at the top. My planned communication with all staff was discussed (weekly blog post updates), and I requested their ideas for these weekly updates. We agreed to have quarterly all-staff meetings, and the team leaders would play roles preparing and delivering the messages. We also decided to conduct monthly new employee orientation sessions, where we would discuss the organization's values and priorities. All team leaders and new staff were expected to participate in these orientation sessions.

Be a humble, learn-it-all, team-player boss, not a narcissistic, know-it-all despot. During management team meetings, sit in the middle of the table, not at the head. Understand the power of your actions. One time, I was in a hurry to get to a meeting with my supervisor as we were wrapping up the weekly team leader meeting. The door accidently slammed shut behind me when leaving the room. Some people would have kept on going, but I went back to let them know: "That wasn't meant to be so loud." Understand the power of your actions, even when unintentional. This lets them know that you care about them.

This is also the time to model the behaviors you want to see. Do not respond to emails at all hours of the night. Do not expect your direct reports to respond to emails at all hours of the night. Do not work excessive hours. Do not expect your team leaders to work excessive hours. Stay home when you are sick, and ask them to do the same. Take vacations, and teach them how to do the same. Establish a family-first prime directive, so when team leaders and their staff are faced with decisions about whether to help a family member, attend a school play, or work, they feel safe to always choose family. I would always say, "Take care of your family and yourself. We have 330 people in our department who will gladly back you up."

Address long-standing roadblocks or problems to set the tone that you are a manager who listens and can actually get things accomplished. Watkins also advises that "addressing problems that your boss cares about will go a long way toward building credibility and cementing your access to resources."[4]

Taking over a troubled organization is harder and more complicated. I found that usually the "good" people are really the "bad" people, and the supposed "bad" people are the "good" people. An organization becomes troubled when leaders are not following best practices. Staff advocating best practices to bad leaders are often labeled as bad people. Troubled organizations can be turned around by unshackling those bad people to implement best practices and letting go of those good people who do not want to change.

For example, David was my direct report. His prior boss had condescendingly nicknamed him "the form filler-outer." When there were surveys to fill out, David was assigned the task. However, I had worked with David 14 years earlier, when he was a client, and I knew he was very talented. In fact, he became our lead negotiator on all major contracts for my organization, and he saved the enterprise millions of dollars. All large-scale contracts negotiated by David benefitted from his intelligence, strategic thinking, creativity, attention to detail, resilience, adaptability, and patience during the negotiation process. I acknowledged David's many tangible contributions in a weekly blog post and observed, "Many organizations have exceptional employees like we do, who go about their work with perseverance and passion. Their focus is to be of service and to contribute to the greater good, and not to toot their own horn. David is one such employee."

I was also part of a new management team at the firm tasked to turn around a $100 million troubled project that was months behind schedule and over budget. Staff was working extremely long hours with no end in sight. They would drag themselves in around nine a.m. and work until dinner. After a two-hour dinner break, they trudged back and worked until ten or eleven p.m. This was not sustainable, and the entire team was demoralized. It was a death march.

Though extremely difficult, we stopped the project for two weeks and asked all the staff to take a vacation. The management team reestimated the remaining work to create more realistic budgets, schedules, and contingencies. A new tool was put in place to accurately track project budget and schedule. We nicknamed the project tracking tool "The Rudder," because we finally knew how to guide the project. In fact, someone found an old white and blue sailboat rudder, and we hung it on the main conference room wall to remind us that we were no longer rudderless. Some of the allegedly good managers turned out to be bad managers who could not adapt and soon left the project. After the project reset, morale dramatically improved as the team began to make real progress and was ultimately successful.

Another aspect of nurturing a safe ecosystem is to help your direct reports address conflicts in a timely manner. Conflict is inevitable. One of my team leaders, Susan, observed, "You understand that management means dealing with conflict. Thank you for not letting conflicts fester." You and your direct reports need conflict management skills and the courage to deal with conflict in the organization. The goal is to better understand what is going on and to constructively work through the conflict. Better solutions can be produced when worked through carefully and respectfully. The authors of *Crucial Conversations: Tools for Talking When the Stakes Are High*, Kerry Patterson, Joseph Grenny, Ron McMillan, and Al Switzler, offer insight into how to "prepare for high-stakes situations, transform anger and hurt feelings into powerful dialogue, make it safe to talk about almost anything, and be persuasive, not abrasive."[5] Dramatic improvements in organizational performance are possible when we foster crucial conversations to air opposing opinions and harness strong emotions in high-stakes situations.

One time, two team leaders in conflict copied me on a fierce email exchange as they hurled opinions and emotions back and forth. They were officed right next to each other. I walked over and called them both into an empty office, closed the door, and said in short, simple words, "From this point forward, you will meet in person to resolve your issues. No more email battles, or I'll throw the email equipment into the street!"

There are at times issues relating to actions, inactions, or opinions of a peer team leader. When my direct reports escalated an issue they had with a peer, I expected them to reach out first to their peer to resolve the issue. Whenever one of my team leaders came to ask me to rescue them and solve their problem with another colleague, I would always ask, "What happened when you talked with them?" It did not take long for my direct reports to learn that they had to work things out together and not come to me to rescue them.

A crazy variation of team leader conflict is triangulation, where one team leader complains to another team leader about a third team leader's actions, inactions, or opinions. Some people do this for weeks and even months unless you, as the manager, step in to stop them. Whenever you witness triangulation, instruct the person who is complaining to talk directly with the person they have an issue with.

It is your responsibility to create a safe work ecosystem and to set the tone for how you want your team to work. First, you'll need to encourage them to offer options to resolve problems. Then, you should give them the benefit of the doubt: Expect, offer, and accept apologies rather than just assigning blame. You can't know how things are going if you don't create a situation for them to tell you: Request feedback, and listen to it. You'll also want to avoid micromanagement: Give your people the space and freedom to do their jobs. Finally, you'll need to understand that, at times, a direct report cannot help with a project or a situation. Don't hold that against them, but do find someone who can help.

Encourage options to resolve problems

Your direct reports are closer to the action to solve problems than you will be as the boss. They are better equipped to gather the information, consult with their staff, and develop viable options to resolve problems. Encourage them to be patient and slow down to understand the root causes of problems before jumping to solutions. In their *HBR* article, Oncken and Wass described the degrees of managerial initiative:

> "There are five degrees of initiative that a direct report can exercise in relation to the boss:

1. Wait until told (lowest initiative);

2. Ask what to do;

3. Recommend, then take action;

4. Act, but advise at once;

5. And act on own, then routinely report (highest initiative)."[6]

Clearly, the first two initiatives should be banned. Initiatives three, four, and five are the best options. Each problem raised to you should be assigned a mutually agreed-upon level of initiative and a time frame to discuss resolution.

There will be times when a direct report asks you to fight a battle on their behalf outside of your area of influence or responsibility. Do not battle over issues that cannot be won. My response to one such request was, "Today, my horoscope says, if you pursue conflict, there will be winners and losers, and they'll be one and the same. Choose peace instead, and you won't have to worry about this anymore." We chose peace.

There will also be times when you do have to help fight a battle on behalf of a direct report when the issue is in your sphere of influence and responsibility. For example, I had a boss who questioned the integrity and motivations of one of my team leads, Lori.

I asked my boss why he had Lori in the penalty box. The message to my supervisor was this: "Lori has survived my two predecessors because of her ability to deliver, her talent, and integrity. I have difficulty reconciling your kudos for me on the tremendous progress of the organization during the past year with your lack of confidence in Lori, who has been a key part of this success. I rely and support Lori without reservation. I ask you to do the same, if you want to make this work. If there are specific instances of past transgressions by Lori, I need to know. If your misgivings are based on my predecessors, I ask for forgiveness so we can move on. I look forward to clearing the air and moving ahead."

In addition, I asked my manager to meet one-on-one with Lori in order to clear the air. I worked with Lori on a script for this meeting. Here are some excerpts from her script: "I want to be of value to the organization and need you to understand and appreciate what I do. I have kept my operations running smoothly in the face of geometric growth. In my 22 years with the organization, I successfully worked with 10 different bosses. I spurned many job offers over the years because of my belief in the mission of our enterprise. I appreciate Brad's trust, guidance, and support. I also need your trust, guidance, and support to meet the daunting challenges ahead."

Afterward, my boss sent this message to me: "I had a great conversation with Lori. We are lucky to have her on our team. Thanks for encouraging the discussion."

Empower your direct reports to be patient and slow down to identify the root causes of problems before offering options to resolve problems. Create a safe work ecosystem by building trusting working relationships with your team leaders, and encourage them to do the same with their teams. Every problem leaving your office should have a mutually agreed initiative level and time frame for resolution. There will also be times when you have to help fight a battle on behalf of a direct report when the issue is in your sphere of influence and responsibility.

Expect, offer, and accept apologies

We live in an imperfect world. You and your direct reports will make mistakes. As Chapman and Thomas explain in *The Five Languages of Apology*, it is the art of apology that counts.[7]

One of my team leaders, Sally, cultivated a friendship with

Ann, a senior financial analyst. Unfortunately, this friendship was based on the thrill of sharing gossip. Ann approached Sally with confidential information regarding a pending personnel action for a peer team leader. Sally reported to me that email rumors from Ann were spreading. I asked Sally to forward the email to me. I also asked the Information Security Office to pull a copy of Ann's original emails on this topic. The content of the two emails did not match. Sally had altered the email from Ann before sending it to me. After I showed her the original email, Sally admitted to altering it.

She said, "I am sorry. I recognize that my actions have broken your trust when I failed to tell you that the email was altered. In the future, all information will be shared openly, and I will always be up front with the information to you, my supervisor."

I accepted her apology and said, "If anyone approaches you with gossip, you must direct them to cease, desist, and get back to work." We agreed that any further lapses in behavior or judgment might result in termination.

Another behavior to look out for as the boss is when a direct report attributes your approval of a decision without you knowing anything about it. This misattribution happened to me several times by different direct reports. Here is an example: "Excellent work! The plan is very well laid out. This has been approved by Brad, so please move forward." The trouble was, not only had I not approved the effort, but I had put a stop to it. After I called the team leader out on her misattribution, she apologized and changed her behavior. As the leader, it was my responsibility to take action, accept the apology, and move forward.

One of my most talented team leaders developed proprietary materials while earning her master's degree on a part-time basis.

She was asked to present some of these ideas and concepts to all the departments reporting to my supervisor. However, one of my supervisor's attorneys attempted to claim ownership of my team leader's intellectual property, so she decided to resign. I apologized for not jumping in sooner to resolve the issue and said, "We are not the first people to work through an intellectual property issue, so no need to rediscover fire, nor reinvent the wheel, or any other cliché that I can come up with at the moment." Her response was, "The dog is sleeping, and I don't want to wake it." She retained her intellectual property and went on to start a successful consulting practice, and we remain good friends.

The world is messy. We make mistakes. Some people do not tell the truth. We need to be ready to expect, offer, and accept apologies.

Request feedback

One-on-one meetings each week with your direct reports offer opportunities to continually ask for feedback. In *The First 90 Days*, Watkins encourages a new boss to meet one-on-one with each member of the inherited team as soon as possible. Watkins offers some sample questions:

- "What are the strengths and weaknesses of our existing strategy?

- What are the biggest challenges and opportunities facing us in the short term?

- What resources could we leverage more effectively?

- How could we improve the way the team works together?

- If you were in my position, what would your priorities be?"[8]

Subsequent one-on-one team leader meetings should foster a continuous dialogue. Your team leads are in the best position to give you open and honest feedback. One of my team leaders advised me to use *we*, not *I* in my weekly blog posts. I followed this great advice for years afterward. Requesting feedback helps to create a safe work ecosystem by demonstrating that you trust and respect the thoughts and opinions of your direct reports.

Let them do their jobs

No one likes to be micromanaged. Give your direct reports the room to make decisions, especially within their respective teams. Hire well, and then entrust the people you've hired.

There will be times when you must help a direct report, even if it means disobeying your boss. For example, if your supervisor asks you or a direct report to do something unethical, refuse to do so and report it to the appropriate company channels. As Sun Tzu advised in *The Art of War* 2,500 years ago, not all instructions are meant to be obeyed: "There are roads that must not be followed, armies which must not be attacked, towns which must not be besieged, positions which must not be contested, commands of the sovereign which must not be obeyed."[9]

Not all orders are meant to be obeyed. You should give your people—and yourself—the freedom to do what is best for them, the project, the customer, and the organization.

Sometimes, a direct report cannot help

You will discover that at times your team leaders do not have the skills, knowledge, or abilities to be successful. For example, I had a candidate who looked great on paper. She had a solid educational background and a work history of relevant roles with increasing responsibilities. During the interview process, she said all the right things, and we extended an offer. Over time, I came to realize that she was very good at managing up, but she micromanaged her team and was not open to their ideas. She also did not work well with the other team leaders. During a mission-critical initiative, she froze when things went dramatically wrong.

The reality was that she was unprepared for the work we'd asked her to do. Yes, we should have figured that out in the hiring process, but that's not always possible. Once we did figure it out, we had no choice but to replace her and either find a new position for her or let her go. Thank goodness she took a job elsewhere. Her successor rebuilt the team and successfully completed this and a number of other mission-critical initiatives.

You can create a safe work ecosystem by understanding the importance of building the team you have inherited. Encourage your team leaders to offer options to resolve problems. Expect, offer, and accept apologies, and ask for feedback. Give them the freedom to do their jobs. And understand that, at times, a direct report cannot help, so find someone who can.

LET THEM KNOW YOU CARE

Just like with your supervisor and your executive leaders, it's crucial to show your direct reports that you care about their success and their teams' success. You'll need to show grit and model the professional will to succeed. You'll also need to understand their goals and aspirations and then recognize and celebrate their successes. To help your direct reports grow, you'll want to ask them to build a variety of long-term business relationships and to build trust with decision-making transparency. Finally, again to help them grow, you'll need to actively invest in their career development.

Grit and modeling the will to succeed

There is always a way to figure out how to best move forward. Have a can-do mindset, and reinforce that attitude in your team. There is always a way to figure out when you appropriately and diligently consider all of your options. "No" is simply not the answer. The coaching for my direct reports was, "Identify the problem, create options, find a solution, and convince others that it's the way to go."

Jim Collins, author of *Good to Great: Why Some Companies Make the Leap . . . and Others Don't,* conducted research over five years that identified 11 good-to-great companies. One of the drivers of good-to-great transformations was leadership.[10] However, these leaders were not egocentric and didn't have extreme personalities. Collins identified the characteristics common to the good-to-great leaders in the article, "Level 5 Leadership: The Triumph of Humility and Fierce Resolve": humility, professional will, ferocious resolve, and the tendency to give credit to others while assigning blame to themselves.[11] The level-5 executive "builds enduring greatness through a paradoxical combination of personal humility plus professional will."[12] Collins provides a number of examples, but Coleman M. Mockler, chief executive officer of Gillette from 1975 to 1991, showed an impressive amount of grit: "Mockler simply would not give in. His placid persona hid an inner intensity, a dedication to making anything he touched the best—not just because of what he would get but because he couldn't imagine doing it any other way."[13]

On my office wall, I inherited a framed quote from the legendary football coach Vince Lombardi: "The spirit, the will to win, and the will to excel—these are the things that endure, and these are the qualities that are so much more important than any of the events that occasion them. The difference between a successful person and others is not a lack of strength, not a lack of knowledge, but rather a lack of will."[14]

One of my best team leaders, Susan, once lamented that she had the wrong degree for leading her team: "I need a psychology degree, not an engineering degree."

I laughed, agreed with her, and asked her to come to my office. I took the Vince Lombardi quote off the wall and gave it to her, knowing she was a ferocious football fan. "Here," I said, "this is yours now. I know you will be successful because you have the professional will to win and excel." Sure enough, Susan had the courage, confidence, strength, smarts, and professional skills to keep her teams moving forward to achieve success on multiple occasions.

You also need to have a sense of humor and not take yourself too seriously. A sense of humor helps you and your team leads put things into perspective. Be able to laugh and move forward.

Another colleague, Jenny, and I were returning home to

Austin from a project in Champaign, Illinois. She was more than eight months pregnant with her first child and was set to go on maternity leave as soon as she returned home. We were on a small commuter jet heading to Chicago's O'Hare International Airport to connect with the last nonstop flight to Austin that night. As we approached the airport for landing, we both looked out the window and were shocked to see towering thunderclouds with lightning hovering above the runways. Soon, we were diverted to Milwaukee to wait out the storm.

"Jenny," I said, "I know you are very uncomfortable. Hang on, and I'll get us a couple of hotel rooms, and we'll fly home in the morning."

Unfortunately, sixty other planes were also diverted to the Milwaukee airport, and there were not enough gates for us to get off the plane. After midnight, we were flown back to O'Hare. We were dismayed to see airport staff setting cots out in the terminal around two in the morning.

I took Jenny's Executive Platinum frequent flyer card and placed it next to mine in front of a gate agent. I do not know what I said, but I knew there was absolutely no way she would be sleeping on a cot in the terminal that night. Even though the airline policy was to not provide lodging due to inclement weather, we soon had vouchers for two airport motel rooms and two first-class tickets on the earliest flight out the next morning. Jenny still refers to this as "the night I spent with Brad Englert."

Demonstrate to your team leaders your grit, humility, and professional will to succeed. Mentor them to identify root causes of problems, form options to resolve problems, find the best solutions, and convince others that's the way to go.

Understand their goals and aspirations

You must take the time to understand the goals and aspirations of your direct reports; otherwise, how will you ever help them achieve these goals? Do they want to be in your position someday? If yes, ask them to serve as the acting boss when you are out of the office. Administer 360-degree reviews to identify their strengths and weaknesses and yours too. A 360-degree review solicits feedback from your supervisor, coworkers, and the people you manage to give you the opportunity to understand how your work is viewed by others in the organization. Set personal development goals each year during the annual review process and track progress. Provide opportunities for your direct reports to present ideas and proposals, and discuss their priorities with your supervisor, which gives your direct reports more visibility and helps to build your boss's confidence in them and your management team.

In the *HBR* article "5 Questions to Help Your Employees Find Their Inner Purpose," Kristi Hedges advises leaders to ask their direct reports the following: "What are you good at doing? What do you enjoy? What feels most useful? What creates a sense of forward momentum? How do you relate to others?"[15] Periodic check-ins asking these questions is one way to help your employees explore and discover their inner purpose. Demonstrating that you care about their success adds to the emotional bank account that you share.

Investment in professional career coaching for your team leaders is an effective way to help them develop new skills and awareness. An independent career coach can have a profound impact. Career coaches can identify unique strengths and areas for growth, develop the patience to work through challenges at the speed needed, provide tools for having crucial conversations, give more perspective and awareness of internal dialogue, and share proven approaches to find common ground and mutual purpose in personal interactions.

One of my team leaders said of her career coach, "Our personalities meshed well, and she's got the type of creative leadership consulting experience that will be very helpful to me." Another team leader said that their career coach helped them to "better understand many things they already knew, often unconsciously, to gain better perspectives on how to manage and improve personal foibles, and to understand that if something is not working, self-reflection is needed. Thank you for getting me a coach. I appreciate and am grateful for the investment in me. The payback has been manyfold already."

Professional career coaches can also provide you with suggestions for how to get the best from your team leaders. Here is an example message to me from a career coach: "Provide opportunities for her to lead and direct others. Provide gentle nurturing. Provide plenty of opportunities for her to act on her own initiative. Make an extra effort to explain how carefully and thoroughly you have considered your decisions."

Seek to understand the goals, aspirations, and inner purpose of your direct reports so that you can help them succeed. Work together to create personal development plans and monitor progress. Employ 360-degree reviews to garner feedback on their strengths and areas for development including yours too. Consider investments in professional career coaches. All these actions will add to your emotional bank account.

Help them build relationships

You and your team leaders must create and nurture authentic business relationships with peers throughout the enterprise and with customers. Set the expectation that, every six to eight weeks, the entire management team will liaise with their peers and external customers at their locations. The purpose of these liaison meetings is to glean information about how well your organization is delivering services, to understand customer priorities, to determine whether your team can help, and to identify unmet business needs. Often, when preparing the agenda for my liaison meetings, I would remember topics to give my peers and customers insight on future initiatives.

In one organization, I had seven team leaders reporting to me. Each of us had from five to 10 peers and customers in the enterprise whom we reached out to in the liaison program. This liaison feedback was discussed in our weekly management meetings. We established and nurtured a strong network of business relationships, which served as our organization's nervous system. We purposely met with people critical of our organization to better understand their concerns. We wanted them inside the tent solving issues with us, not outside throwing rocks. We gathered good and bad feedback, garnered input on team leader performance, and defused rumors that we could address. We also built up goodwill by getting out of our offices and letting people know that we gave a damn.

In addition, the liaison program encouraged my direct reports to work as a team. They had to know the elevator speech for all of their peer team leader's major projects, forcing all team leads to learn and care about everyone's success.

Just as I did for my one-on-one meetings with my manager, I

would solicit topics for my liaison meetings with high-level executives. Often I would invite my team leads to my liaison meetings to give them greater executive-level visibility and to help them hear firsthand about those executive leaders' needs, concerns, and priorities. This inclusive approach helped to improve communication countless times and fostered executive-level trust and confidence in my management team's ability to deliver outstanding service.

Here is an example of an email exchange between one of my team leaders and a peer customer executive. My team leader said, "Your team brought their magic to the table. Thanks to their help, hard work, sage advice, and expertise—which we could not do without—it looks like the date is doable."

The customer executive responded: "Thank you for those kind words. I'll share them with my folks. Now my turn, I want you to be sure and understand that it takes two to tango, and our ability to work successfully with your organization has been substantially increased as a result of your energy and leadership."

I would also get feedback on my team leaders during my liaison meetings: "I support Lori and believe she is an asset to your organization. She's a professional whose word I can trust. She has managed to deliver on projects in spite of some openly hostile customers."

Rumors can be quickly addressed. One of my team leaders was falsely accused of not supporting a new program, and misinformation was spreading about her views. I reached out to my peer liaison executive responsible for this program and said, "Sara has been working tirelessly to make sure your program is successful for both of our organizations. She and I are disappointed about the rumors." My peer executive agreed and put a stop to the rumors.

You and your team leaders must establish and nurture authentic business relationships with peers and customers throughout the enterprise. The liaison program establishes a nervous system for your organization and builds trust and goodwill.

Recognize and celebrate success

You need to let your team leaders know when they are doing an exceptional job. Take the time to pause and say thank you. There are plenty of opportunities for expressing authentic appreciation: "Hey Mike, excellent job in the meeting with my boss this afternoon."

Here is my note to another team leader: "Hi, Mary. A high-level customer executive sought me out in a meeting today to let me know that you are top notch. Thank you for making our organization look good." I copied my supervisor to give Mary some positive visibility. The boss replied, "Excellent! Thanks for representing us so well, Mary . . . You are top notch."

Mary responded, "Thank you both. We have a great group of people here as employees and customers. Everyone is trying to do the right thing. I am having a great time here and love it!"

A peer colleague copied me on this email: "Sara, thank you for your preparation and thoughts in today's session. You brought a lot to the table." My reply was, "Sara thinks strategically and plans years ahead. Then she hires really good people, holds them accountable, and delivers on time and on budget."

Celebrate successes by treating your direct reports to lunch, one-on-one and with the entire management team. Breaking bread together is an effective way to build strong working relationships with your team leaders. Recognize major achievements with a cash bonus when you can. Reward your direct reports with tickets to a concert or sporting event that they may enjoy. My wife and I are Friends of Austin City Limits, and our annual donation comes with tickets to multiple tapings, which I often share with my team. One of my team leaders said, "Thank you so much for the tickets. The evening was just awesome. I've been to some great shows, concerts, etc., but this was near the top of the list of events that I've ever attended."

You can also nominate a direct report for a professional award. Professional associations have award nomination processes. Unbeknownst to Phillip, one of my team leaders, I enlisted the support of his team's managers and staff to draft a nomination for an international award. I shared a copy of the nomination with him, and here was his thank you to his team: "The nomination was a surprise and quite humbling. But more than anything, it was so enjoyable just to read and reflect back on where we have come from over the last five years. From my perspective, I feel like we have already won."

Phillip did, in fact, win the international manager-of-the-year award. He said, "I greatly appreciate your support. The award ceremony took place at a luncheon in Las Vegas, with about 1,000 other geeks. It was an honor to be recognized and such an honor for our team."

Recognizing and celebrating success lets your direct reports know that you truly care for them and their teams.

Build trust

It is important to explain to your team leaders why you are making a decision and why you are not making a decision. Transparency with your decision-making builds trust. By sharing your reasoning, team leaders can offer different perspectives that will help shape the solution.

Not deciding is also a decision. There are circumstances where not making a decision is the best course of action. This type of decision-making is called "intentional foot dragging." Your direct reports may need more time to define a problem or gather supporting data. There is no need to run headfirst to a solution before truly understanding what the root causes are. Encourage your team leaders to be patient. At times, the problem may work itself out for unforeseen reasons after pausing.

Sometimes an organization might not be ready for a change. A client of mine once asked if we could delay the start of a project by three months so their new executive could gain their bearings. "Of course!" was the answer. This type of flexibility shows and builds trust with your team and your customers.

There are also times when you make a recommendation to one of your team leads and the recipient decides not to heed your advice. Based on years of experience, you know how things will most likely go wrong. The most frustrating part is when you see in your mind this imaginary truck barreling down the road toward them, you ask them again to step off the road, and then "BAM," they are flattened! There is nothing you can do. Welcome to one of the joys of management. Building trust helps you avoid this scenario but won't completely stop it.

One of the most difficult types of decision-making is to pause or stop something that is not working. Many organizations are terrible at stopping work, even when it is clearly wasting time and money. For example, you and your direct report have invested in a new initiative and you are anticipating a dramatic, hockey-stick increase in benefits. When these benefits do not pan out, it is human nature to keep going and not pull the plug. When you have the experience of suspending and resetting a $100 million project, stopping smaller projects is easy. It is never a good idea to keep spending good money after bad, and making the right choice will build trust in your decision-making skills.

In their *Harvard Business Review* article "Start Stopping Faster," Darrell Rigby, Sarah Elk, and Steve Berez say, "There is another way." Organizations can start stopping things faster by focusing on three things: "[making] more decisions reversible, [making] work more visible, and [overpowering] fear."[16] If you approach decisions as reversible, "a company won't have to live with bad consequences for very long."[17] More visibility helps to "uncover valuable initiatives, recognize the people pushing them, and accelerate their progress."[18] Overpower fear by "reducing the cost of stopping projects" by breaking them into smaller, more manageable chunks of work.[19]

One of my direct reports selected a software solution, but he was not sure who would use the solution. He did not factor in the cost of the equipment, personnel support, or ongoing maintenance. After I explained the reasoning for stopping this effort, he was not happy, but he understood why, and there were no regrets from me.

Explain how you make decisions. Transparent decision-making with your direct reports builds trust and improves the quality of the solutions.

Invest in skill development

An organization's greatest expenses are employee salaries and benefits, so investing in the career development of your direct reports and staff is imperative. You must work with your team leaders to map out annual training plans. During the year, you and your team leaders are accountable for ensuring that the skill development goals outlined in training plans are achieved. I have seen situations where people say they are "too busy" for skill development, which is ridiculous. It is unfair to both you and your direct reports to cancel career development due to lack of planning ahead. By being proactive, absences can be effectively managed. You and your team leaders will demonstrate the importance of career development in your organization when you take the time to do so.

In *The 7 Habits of Highly Effective People*, Stephen R. Covey describes the importance of skill development as habit seven: "sharpening the saw." He describes this scene:

> "Suppose you were to come upon someone in the woods working feverishly to saw down a tree.
>
> 'What are you doing?' you ask.
>
> 'Can't you see?' comes the impatient reply. 'I'm sawing down this tree.'
>
> 'How long have you been at it?'
>
> 'Over five hours.'
>
> 'Well, why don't you take a break for a few minutes and sharpen that saw?'
>
> 'I don't have time to sharpen the saw,' the man says emphatically. 'I'm too busy sawing!'"[20]

You and your direct reports are responsible for proactively planning and achieving career development goals. It is a weakness—not a strength—to neglect or postpone skill development.

This investment will return benefits many times over, including the increased engagement of your leadership team.

Here is what a peer colleague said about my leadership team built over eight years: "Wow, they are great—professional, articulate, knowledgeable, personable, logical, and so willing to help."

Let your direct reports know that you care about their success and the success of their teams. Demonstrate grit and lead by example. Seek to understand their goals, aspirations, and inner purpose. Ask them to build a variety of long-standing business relationships. Recognize and celebrate success. Build trust with transparent decision-making, and invest in skill development. Creating and nurturing authentic business relationships with your direct reports is your responsibility and is critical for the success of your organization.

KEY TAKEAWAYS

- Articulate the organization's values, set expectations, and establish mutual accountability.

- Create a safe work ecosystem.

- Let direct reports know you care about their success and their team's success.

Chapter 4

RELATIONSHIPS WITH ALL OF YOUR STAFF

WHEN YOU HAVE THE UNIQUE OPPORTUNITY TO lead an organization, establish the values of the organization and set expectations with all of your staff as you did with your direct reports. Seek to create a safe work ecosystem, especially if you inherit a wounded workgroup. Build a work environment where honesty and trust will thrive. Let all your staff know you care about their success and the well-being of the organization.

You'll begin to change the culture by establishing the values of the organization. This is a crucial step to ensure that everyone is on the same page and working toward the same goals. Then, you'll need to make sure they understand what is expected of them. This is similar to how you need to understand your supervisor's expectations and to clarify your own expectations for your direct reports. If people don't know what's expected, they can't meet—or exceed—those expectations. Finally, let your people know that the relationship is a two-way street. Leadership is not issuing top-down commands; it is an ongoing conversation.

Changing the culture

In *The First 90 Days*, Michael Watkins offers proven approaches to avoid common pitfalls as you transition into a new leadership role. He describes how to prepare to take charge, accelerate your learning, secure early wins, and achieve alignment with your strategy, structure, systems, skills, and culture. In addition, he emphasizes the importance of building the team you have inherited and how to change it.[1]

Start with the expectation that all your staff are doing their best to achieve the organizational goals, and then showcase the new values. Short weekly blog posts to update your staff is a proven method to communicate the values of the organization. Each week, you can focus on the specific values you need to convey.

For example, in an early blog post, I shared my approach to decision-making as follows: "Data driven and customer focused. If you have an idea that improves the customer experience and is supported by data, 99 times out of 100 it will be approved."

Weekly blog posts are a good way to show support and establish honesty and trust as key values. They are particularly effective if you inherit an organization where the grapevine of gossip prevails. Once, I made the mistake of depending on my team leads to convey these important messages to their staff. Some of them did share these aspirational values with their teams, but I was surprised and disappointed that several did not. Those team leaders did not understand the importance of communicating and modeling these values to their teams, while others enjoyed the heady power of withholding the information.

Quarterly all-staff meetings are another important tool to deliver and reinforce organizational values and priorities. All-staff meetings should be hybrid: in-person for most staff, live-streamed for those working remotely, and recorded for employees who are unable to leave their posts or who work night shifts. These events are great opportunities for everyone to hear directly from their executive leaders, to meet people outside of their groups, to exchange experiences, to hear directly from customers, and to discuss ways to better meet customer needs and improve service delivery. Staff should be asked to sit with people from other teams and participate in group discussions, which will foster interactions between people throughout the organization.

Conducting monthly new employee orientation sessions is another technique to embed your organization's values and priorities. All team leads and new staff are expected to participate in these orientation sessions. Keep track of who attends to be sure that all team leaders and new employees participate. I found that, on more than one occasion, a new employee was "too busy" to attend, so they were invited to the next orientation session—no exceptions. We also assigned guides for each new employee. The guides were experienced peers who our new employees could reach out to for help navigating their new organization.

Here is an example of a wounded organization that I inherited and how it was addressed. The prior leader of the organization was egocentric, and his three direct reports often disagreed with each other. These open rifts at the top of the organization caused the 11 team leaders who worked for the three direct reports to be whipsawed with conflicting priorities, procedures, and direction. One employee said, "What senior management did was always 'right,' and if staff questioned it, retaliation followed. Senior management thought that customers did not deserve communication or consideration."

This organization's reactive culture rewarded firefighting. When something went wrong, heroes stepped up to save the day. This organization's culture valued gurus and experts, without a customer service ethic, which made it difficult for customers to approach the department for assistance and get the help they needed after they made contact. Things often went wrong, because there was little proactive planning and no standard policies and practices on what should be done when things did go wrong. Much of the equipment was old, some beyond its end of life, and there was no capital budget for life cycle replacement and no operating budget to keep equipment running smoothly. Customers were often surprised by outages, staff training budgets were cut, and staff morale was at an all-time low.

In stark contrast to the positive self-assessment by that leadership team, their customers perceived that the organization was arrogant and not always truthful. The organization did not have a high level of trust or the respect of external customers. There was a lot of dictating of decisions to the customers. Only a small number of individuals or teams were cited by customers as being responsive, knowledgeable, and customer focused. Customer service requests were managed differently by various groups in the organization. Ten different customer request tracking tools were being used to various degrees, which offered little insight to systemic cross-team issues. Even when customers strongly wanted to use a service, determining how to start the service was not easy or straightforward. Mistrust also stemmed from poor customer engagement, a lack of follow-through, inflexibility, and instances of unprofessional behavior on the part of some staff. One employee who supported a mission-critical service refused to answer his phone when there were outages. Perceived and documented inefficiencies and a top-heavy management structure led to low levels of service and higher costs. A lack of transparency on how rates were developed for some services also eroded customer trust.

The first step was to seek organizational efficiencies. The layers of management were reduced throughout the organization by adjusting the management span of control to eliminate situations with one manager to only one or two staff. The senior management team was reduced from 14 to one executive leader and seven team leader positions, which freed up significant recurring funding to meet long-standing needs. During the first two years, three of the remaining seven team leaders were replaced.

We then created multiyear capital and operating budgets. In order to build transparency and trust with customers and clarify the services provided, all services went through a zero-based budgeting process. Zero-based budgeting is a clean-slate, bottom-up approach to justify all expenses so funds can be redirected to advance the department's priorities. All rates were developed by the central accounting group and reviewed by customer oversight committees. We established expectations regarding the time frames for responding to customer requests. One model was selected to manage customer relationships, which were tracked in one system. Service-level agreements (SLAs) were set for services, and metrics were published on the organization's website to establish accountability. Meeting SLAs, customer feedback, and improvements in service quality were incorporated into the employee performance evaluation process.

As described in chapter 3, "Relationships with Direct Reports," we established these new values for the organization:

- Put family first.

- Deliver high-quality services.

- Foster customer partnerships.

- Establish understanding, trust, and accountability.

- Make data-driven, innovative, customer-focused decisions.

- Facilitate collaboration, cooperation, and communication.

These values were prominently displayed on the organization's website and reinforced to all staff via quarterly meetings and weekly blog posts. Orientation sessions for all new employees were scheduled every month so they could learn about these organizational values, ask questions, and meet the management team leaders.

The benefits of these changes were to build a disciplined, service-oriented culture where there was none; to establish understanding and accountability for services delivered; to increase efficiencies in the organization to fund capital and operating needs; to demonstrate the ability to collaborate, communicate, and follow through on service commitments; and to establish trust with customers leading to increased adoption of cost-effective services. We encouraged staff at all levels to build strong working relationships with their customer counterparts.

Actively listen to your staff and customers, and then set the expectations for the future of the organization. Reinforce these values in frequent communications, the organization's website, quarterly all-staff meetings, job postings, and orientations. It's crucial if you want to create a culture of customer service and discipline. Do not depend on vital communications to be passed down through the ranks; it just doesn't happen.

Clarify expectations

Show staff who you are and what you expect from your team. That includes caring for your people and showing them—through your actions—what you value.

Every flu season, this message would be sent to the entire organization: "Stay healthy, and please stay home if you are sick. Don't try to be a hero. Showing up at work when you are sick is not heroic or a considerate thing to do. Trust us. We will cover for you."

The second week leading a large transformational program, I met for the first time with Mark, the manager of one of the teams, along with his junior team leads. He did not have an agenda. I said that we could go ahead and meet that day without an agenda but to please bring one the next week. The next week, we convened, and I asked Mark for a copy of the agenda. He barked at one of his direct reports, "Jones, I told you to bring an agenda!" Jones's eyes bugged out, and he was terrified. Once again, I stepped in and said we could continue to meet and asked for an agenda for all future meetings.

When the meeting finished, I asked Mark to join me in the rose garden adjacent to the building. My direct reports knew that if I invited them to visit the rose garden, it could be to admire and smell the blooms (positive feedback) or to be pricked by a thorn (constructive coaching).

I said, "Mark, you are the manager, not Jones. I expect you to create the agenda each week. Blaming Jones for your miscue in front of everyone was very unfair to him. Please don't do it again."

Jane, the manager who soon replaced Mark, found Jones to be an outstanding consultant. She raised the expectations for her entire team to produce higher-quality work and to be more professional at the client site. When one of Jane's consultants was irritating the client by acting overconfident and curt, she summarily dispatched him to the local office with his head spinning. Jane's decisive action captured everybody's attention.

We addressed Clyde, an employee who did not answer his phone, by documenting two subsequent occasions when he did not answer his phone when the mission-critical service he was primarily responsible for was not working. "We expect you to prioritize emergency calls," we said. "You must be attentive to emergency calls."

Clyde agreed to forward his office phone to his cell phone to be sure to answer calls as they came in. Thankfully, Clyde resigned soon after. We assigned his responsibilities to a trusted employee and provided backup resources to eliminate this single point of failure, which never should have been established in the first place.

You are responsible for clearly setting expectations and taking corrective actions when these expectations are not met. Work with your team leaders to establish policies and practices for the organization to clarify customer expectations, set service-level agreements, and build a customer service–oriented culture. These policies and practices will help your staff and your customers create a shared understanding of what to expect from each other.

Communication is a two-way street

One of the most important benefits of sending weekly updates is the opportunity for all staff to be able to reply directly to you with their thoughts, corrections, and ideas for future communications. In addition to offering weekly blog post updates to all the staff in your organization, you can also distribute the content widely to external customers and peers and influencers to keep them informed, improve transparency, and receive their feedback. Here is feedback from a peer of mine: "I really like your weekly updates. You do a great job communicating with your huge team this way, keeping their eyes focused on the big picture, and helping them understand why it's important."

In one blog post, we recognized staff who received service awards. Three employees had served for 10 years, seven had served for 15 years, and nine employees had served between 15 and 45 years.

Helen sent the following message to me in response: "Thank you for attending the awards ceremony in support of your staff and acknowledging the employee recognitions in this week's blog post. Your latest update was amazing and really empowering; however, it has come to my attention that some of our employees have had to wait weeks or even months to finally receive their service award certificates and pins. That's not a proper way to honor loyal and dedicated service. Would you please look into the matter?"

My reply was, "Thank you, Helen. I was not aware this was happening and totally agree. We will fix it, pronto." From that point forward, the management team worked to ensure that all the service awards were distributed in a timely manner.

Fostering two-way communication brought this issue to light. I would never have known about the delay if communication went only from the leadership down to the staff.

After describing an enterprise-wide pilot program, George sent this feedback: "Thanks for sending the weekly update on the upcoming pilot program. If possible, could you please elaborate on the involvement of our department to alleviate unnecessary confusion and worrying?" My reply was: "Thank you for your suggestion, George. It is much appreciated. I will elaborate on the involvement of our organization in the pilot program in next week's blog post."

LuAnn, an external customer, sent me this message regarding a major project described in a weekly update: "When I first heard of this project, I was terrified about the prospect, thinking it would be incredibly time consuming and an absolute headache. Much to my surprise, it was neither. Working with Alice was a delight, and her team was professional, courteous, knowledgeable, and committed to helping my staff make the transition as seamlessly as possible. I am singing your organization's praises. Thanks again for making this such an easy process."

It is always good to hear from our external customers. Throughout the year, customer feedback can be shared in the weekly updates. Your staff needs to know that customers really appreciate their work. Customer kudos reinforce the positive impact that outstanding customer service makes in people's lives. This positive customer feedback is like a flywheel that builds momentum toward ever-increasing customer service.

My last two years with the firm, I had the opportunity to manage a virtual team of 95 professionals who helped transition clients in all industries to a variety of outsourcing services. The team members were experts in human resources, communications, project management, change management, and technology. They lived all over the US and Canada. Weekly staffing calls with the senior executives provided an opportunity for all of us to understand the capabilities of every team member and identify opportunities for them to serve in stretch roles and develop deeper skills. We conducted a skills analysis exercise to identify growth potentials and gaps. Staffing arrangement agreements were created at the beginning of each project by all assigned staff that documented their role expectations, accountability, approximate roll-off dates, vacation, and training plans. These agreements helped set the expectations for the staff and for our clients.

I also dedicated time to go on Winnebago tours to all the client sites to get feedback from the client leadership and my team members: California, New Jersey, Georgia, Texas, New York, Illinois, Michigan, North Carolina, and British Columbia. My goal was to show my support and be accessible and approachable to the client executives and staff at all levels on my team. According to my 360-degree reviews, my Winnebago tours were often cited and appreciated by team members because I asked for feedback on important aspects of the work and their careers. The team also met in person twice a year to build a culture of cooperative working relationships between team members, so it would be easier for them to reach out for help from someone with a different skill set.

Communication must be a two-way street. Your staff must feel safe to let you know what is and is not working. With this feedback, issues can be addressed quickly, which builds trust and adds to the emotional bank accounts. Cultivating a two-way relationship with your staff keeps you from flying blind. When starting a new role leading an organization, you need to establish and promulgate the values of the organization. Just like your direct reports, all staff must clearly understand what is expected of them and understand that this relationship is a two-way street.

CREATE A SAFE WORK ECOSYSTEM

Just as you did as a supervisor, as the leader of your organization, you need to build a safe, secure, productive, and respectful work environment. Start by encouraging open and honest communication. You and your team leaders must clearly communicate your requirements and expectations. Share important information accurately and quickly, and let the staff know that it is okay to express contrary viewpoints. Promote teamwork and cooperation, and seek to understand and address your staff's concerns, issues, and problems. Provide training to all staff members on the responsible use of social media and email and to increase the sensitivity to issues of equality, sexual harassment, and sexual misconduct in the workplace. Be very clear: "We all expect and deserve a safe, secure, and respectful work environment."

It is also acceptable to show your vulnerability. I have profound hearing loss in my left ear, so I let people know this whenever we first meet. Thereafter, people would ask, "Am I sitting on the correct side?" My reply: "It is always my job to be sure you are sitting on my right side so I can hear you."

You and your team leaders need to defend your staff from bullies. George, a longtime employee, became agitated and began shouting at Maggie, which created an uncomfortable and hostile work environment. Maggie's manager immediately worked with George's team leader and a human resources manager to document the outburst and create a performance improvement plan. George's supervisor wrote: "We met to discuss your performance appraisal that had an overall rating of 'needs improvement.' Specifically, you were told you need to work on your interpersonal skills and communicate in a responsible and professional manner. You were directed to stop communicating by shouting or being verbally abusive." This quick action put an abrupt stop to George's inappropriate behavior.

We also conducted annual disaster-recovery tabletop exercises—ice storm, network outage, cybersecurity threat, and hurricane scenarios—with all the team leaders and their key staff in my department and included several of my peer colleagues from other departments. We randomly selected participants to be silent. We wanted them to observe, and participants knew this individual could not be contacted, which might happen in a real crisis. We added random information during the event. Sometimes it was good information, and other times it was meaningless information that diverted attention from the problem. At each event, we selected a new incident commander; it was always fun when that individual was surprised to be named the incident commander. Monitors fanned out to help the teams connect the dots. These tabletop exercises created a safe work environment for the organization to learn how to always be looking for ways to improve. The key lesson learned was that it is okay to fail and make mistakes if your overarching goal is to improve. The organization's culture changed to embrace this safe work environment.

The war for water—you have to fight for your team

Soon after some gut-wrenching right-sizing of the organization, I met with my supervisor, who was the chief financial officer. The painful elimination of layers of management freed up millions of dollars in recurring savings, which were redirected to the first-ever capital budget. We also saved more than $6 million when replacing a major mission-critical piece of equipment. When he suggested that I should no longer expense bottled water or coffee for my office, I laughed because I thought he was joking. He was dead serious. This small expense was deemed too excessive. My office was located in a building built in 1962, so there were concerns about the quality of the water due to the lead pipes. So, for the next eight years, I paid for and personally delivered the bottled water and coffee for the staff, customers, and vendors who came to meet with me.

You don't always win, but you have to try. The war for water escalated. He wanted me to stop expensing the $700 monthly water service for the rest of my staff. About 330 employees in the organization were officed in buildings built in 1932, 1951, 1960, and 1962. The tap water in the 1951 building was cloudy and contained floating rust-colored particles. The CFO also had staff in the 1932 building, but his other direct report, Frank, established a water club for his team. Staff had to pay into the water club account to be able to drink safe, purified water. Instead of paying for monthly water service for their staff, Frank wanted to bring our department down to his miserly level of staff support to make it "fair."

I deflected multiple requests to cut this cost and intentionally dragged my feet for eight years. We fought this stupid water war until the next CFO finally squashed approval of the water funding out of spite. My last expense request had this justification: "This is a health-related expense, especially in the legacy buildings. Denial of this small, health-related benefit will be seen by staff as mean-spirited and would further reduce employee morale, especially in light of many years with no salary increases. Also, productivity will be lost as 330 staff will need to leave the workplace to purchase their own safe-to-drink water." My heartfelt request was summarily denied.

At my retirement party, my staff presented me with a water cooler and a jug of purified water to memorialize this eight-year internecine water war, and we all had a good laugh. Later, filtered water fountains were installed in some—but not all—of the buildings.

As the leader of your organization, you are responsible for creating a safe work ecosystem, and although I didn't win the multiyear water war, my team knew I was fighting for them. That increased trust and showed them that I genuinely valued them and their health. Demonstrate that you truly care for your employees above yourself.

When I retired, Susan said, "You showed up at an interesting time, full of upheaval, and it's true that I didn't think much of the 'new administration' when you arrived. The years that followed showed me differently, and I've come to understand that you care about this place and the people as much or more than anyone around here."

Be curious, open, and learn from people throughout the organization

Just like in your previous business relationships, as the leader of an organization, you are responsible for creating an environment that encourages employee input from all levels to solve problems. They know the details on the ground better than you ever will. Organize events, such as quarterly all-staff meetings, to discuss major challenges and problems in order to generate options for possible solutions and solicit opinions. Show appreciation for the input. Encourage a spirit of continuous improvement within the organization. Be approachable and visible in the workplace. Ask people what roadblocks or problems they are encountering, and ask them to suggest options to resolve the problems. Set the expectation that, when a problem is identified at all levels, root causes should be found, and options for resolution should be created and raised to the management team.

One tradition of mine was to walk the floor to visibly show support before leaving work each day and informally visit with my direct reports and their team members. This technique is "management by wandering around." I would ask staff what they were working on and whether they had any roadblocks. Often, I would encourage them to go home, just as I was doing.

Earlier, I described a manager who had the mantra, "There's no money!" The result was almost everyone stopped asking for the resources that they knew were needed to support the enterprise services. Those brave enough to ask for resources were punished.

The employees were stressed knowing that the equipment was far beyond its useful life. Only after catastrophic failures did the boss fund the replacement equipment. The employees' morale plummeted as enterprise services failed. My new management team asked the staff to identify equipment vulnerabilities, and funds were reprioritized to replace the aging infrastructure and to dramatically reduce the risks of failure. Proactive planning based on input from the entire organization led to increased customer satisfaction and improved employee morale.

We often leveraged all-staff meetings to seek ideas to improve customer service. All-staff meetings are a great opportunity for everyone to get to know people from outside their own groups, exchange experiences, focus on ways to meet our customers' needs, and improve service delivery. You'll hear from many of your people new ideas that you would not see without asking in these meetings. When your organization invests time to discuss ways to better meet the needs of our customers and values continuous improvement, the results will outshine any result of top-down command-and-control leadership.

After one such meeting, Carol sent this note: "I wanted to tell you that, as I was participating in the all-hands meeting, I really felt that I was part of something big. Week to week, we are launching, improving, or changing something. It was good to reflect with you on our accomplishments and our efforts to improve customer service. I want you to know that I am so excited to be here. Four years ago, you asked me to stay, and I did, and I don't regret it. I have learned so much and laughed and cried so much."

Establish an environment that encourages employee input from all levels to solve problems. Do not kill the messenger, because no more messengers will show up at your door. Instead, be sure your messengers know that you need and appreciate their ideas.

Embrace apologies

We all work in fields that will have problems, complications, mistakes, and malfunctions caused by human error and technical failures. It is a given, and how your organization responds to these inevitable challenges is critical. It is important to establish a protocol when things go wrong:

- Identify the root cause(s) of the problem.

- Alert the relevant parties.

- Apologize by expressing regret, accepting responsibility, describing what is being done to address the problem.

- Create a plan to avoid the problem in the future, genuinely repent, and request forgiveness.

- Thank everyone for their patience and goodwill.

At times, you will encounter people who are suspicious of your organization based on past transgressions. I have experienced someone complaining about a problem caused by my department that happened more than a decade earlier. They made it sound like it had happened yesterday! Listening and empathy are the keys to a successful response, along with taking the time to validate what you hear and offering a sincere and positive, solution-oriented approach. In certain instances, simply ask for forgiveness: "You are right. That past behavior was bad. That employee is no longer with my department. I am truly sorry. Please forgive the past, and give the organization a chance to help. Let's move on. It is time for us to focus on the future."

Within your organization, you may find similar long-standing transgressions and feuds. Set this expectation: "You may have been wronged by another team or person in the past. Trust me: You will be happier if you clear your mind and focus on the future. It is time to move on."

In *The Five Languages of Apology*, Chapman and Thomas aptly describe the art of the apology. The great news is that it can be learned, and the proven techniques can be shared with your entire organization.[2]

Request feedback

Three-hundred-sixty-degree feedback tools are a great way to gain insights on what you are doing well, what you should continue doing, and what you should stop doing. These tools, however, should not be used for appraising performance. Over the course of my career, I have benefited from the feedback from several of these reviews.

There are a number of 360-degree tools available. The firm developed a leadership survey that provided feedback from customers, bosses, direct reports, and the staff regarding each team leader's general leadership attributes, how well the team leader developed their people, how well they created value for their clients and the firm, how well they performed as a business operator, how well they performed as a career counselor, as well as open comments by the raters. The resulting report also provided peer benchmarks for all people at each level in each country. In order to get the most out of this feedback, two job aides were created that offered practical ideas for improving leadership effectiveness and that served as a template to help build a self-development action plan for each leader at every level.

Here is the actual feedback from one 360-degree review after 15 years with the firm:

"Doing well: 'You encourage open and honest communications, develop teamwork and cooperation, work with the team to meet deadlines and solve problems, share credit and recognition for team success, give fair and timely performance appraisals, provide informal feedback during the course of an engagement, encourage team members to determine best methods for achieving tasks, seek to fully understand contrary views before stating an opinion, and recognize and show appreciation for positive contributions of team members.'

"Continue doing: 'Encourage communication at all levels via email and group meetings. Give positive feedback by just walking around to talk with analysts and consultants to see how they are doing. Straightforward honest and open communication on how things are going, especially focusing on solutions and changes to improve versus dwelling on historical issues. Shares information with me and involves me in the decision-making process, provides direction and advises as needed. Provides insight into the overall strategy for customer success to help us understand the ultimate goals and steps to getting there. Meets one-on-one with managers (lunch, dinner) to see how things are going and just talk about stuff, which helps establish relationships and lets us know he is paying attention and really cares about what is going on.'

"Stop doing: 'Please stop interrupting others who are talking; let them complete their thoughts. Don't give the impression that you are listening but have the answer anyhow. Spend more time listening versus talking. Provide feedback directly and not through others. Be more sensitive to balancing work and personal priorities. Spend more time with your people to get to know them as a person versus a resource that is there to accomplish work. Stop cancelling single-day events away from the project site that can help consultants build connections with other professionals in their local office.'"

I heeded all this advice and strived to get better. Above all, more listening than talking and better balancing work with personal priorities has served me well.

The Covey Leadership Center has a 360-review tool. The Seven Habits Profile provides you with information on how others perceive your performance in the areas of Covey's seven habits (be proactive, begin with the end in mind, put first things first, think win–win, seek first to understand then to be understood, synergy, and sharpen the saw).[3] The resulting profile helps you understand the feedback and create an action plan for improvement.

A year and a half after I became the leader of a large department, we employed the Lominger VOICES 360 process to gain insight into how our team leaders, peers, customers, bosses, and others viewed our skill levels for crucial competencies. The goal was to provide team leaders and me the opportunity to build development plans based on current and future skill levels. We shared the aggregate results with all staff and our external customers. It was heartening to see "integrity and trust" and "a customer focus" as our top-two-rated aggregate skills. Although it had not been easy, we had evidence that real, positive cultural change happened in the department, and there were significant and measurable successes. The 360-degree feedback also indicated where we had areas to improve. It was clear that we needed to build deeper skills in "planning and priority setting, understanding others, and building effective teams." In the following years, team leaders worked with staff and customers to develop methodologies, templates, processes, and procedures to build these skills and capabilities.

It is always helpful to know what you are doing well, what you should continue doing, and what you should stop doing. As painful as it is, do not overly fixate on negative feedback. Make a conscious effort to address the constructive criticism and to develop new skills to become an even better leader.

Give them freedom

Just like with your direct reports, you can never be the primary problem solver for your organization. Enable decision-making autonomy for your team leaders, and give them the mental space and freedom to generate solutions to challenges and problems with input from their team members. Those employees closest to the work will have pragmatic insights leavened with experience. Your team members should be involved in goal-setting processes, setting deadlines, identifying and raising problems, proposing alternatives to resolve problems, and articulating what additional resources may be needed to meet goals and deadlines. Ask for creative ideas, and empower your staff to take responsibility to make things right when they are faced with problems.

Understand who can and cannot help

At times, you will need to seek help from outside your organization to solve problems or address challenges. This help may be from other parts of the enterprise or outside the enterprise.

Ray was a manager for the team that processed payroll for a large enterprise. Every time payroll was run, there were errors. In frustration, I blurted out, "We have shot ourselves in the feet so many times that we have Swiss cheese feet!" Working with Ray and his team, we discovered that James was manually processing payroll twice a month at night and often worked until three or four in the morning after working all day. Obviously, James was exhausted, and human error was inevitable. So, we added two new support staff to process payroll on a night shift, which dramatically reduced the errors and addressed an internal audit risk. Then we retained a small team from outside the enterprise to implement an automatic scheduling tool for payroll processing, which cured our embarrassing case of Swiss cheese feet.

As the leader of your organization, you will need to build a safe, secure, productive, and respectful work ecosystem. This will build trust in your team and enable you to focus on the bigger picture for the organization.

LET THEM KNOW YOU CARE

There are several actions that prove to all the staff in your organization that you care and are committed to their success. First, like at every other level of your career, you're going to need grit and the will to succeed. You will need to model those features for your team and help them build those skills. Next, you'll again need to understand your employees' goals and aspirations. Your job is to help them build toward those goals, even if it means them going elsewhere. Ask them to create and nurture authentic business relationships so they are connecting with their peers and customers. Always communicate and celebrate their successes; this is a simple and immediate way to communicate their importance to you and to the organization. Make sure you are continuing your focus on transparent decision-making. Finally, invest in training and career development; this again shows that you are helping your team build toward something bigger for themselves and for the enterprise.

Grit and the will to succeed

Remember that it's important to demonstrate grit to your boss. It is equally important to convey to your staff the need to demonstrate grit in their delivery of services. In *Grit*, Angela Duckworth posits that it is not just talent but grit that matters most in achieving success.[4] And also remember the characteristics common to good-to-great leaders: humility, professional will, ferocious resolve, and the tendency to give credit to others while assigning blame to themselves.

At the firm, true grit is exemplified with a can-do mindset and a willingness to take risks. According to *Values. Driven. Leadership: The History of Accenture*, the can-do mindset is the key ingredient in the firm's "special sauce: a mixture of confidence, drive, and the willingness to commit the resources to get the job done."[5]

This was a message to all staff in one of my organizations: "As I think about the challenges we face to modernize information technology in our enterprise, Duckworth's research and insights are useful and strengthening. On many fronts, we are working together to ensure the success of our modernization efforts. There is no going back, no quitting. We are progressing forward to implement improvements that will significantly contribute to our enterprise. Grit will help us achieve our goals. When the going gets tough—and it will—the ability to endure is one of the best and most important ways to contribute to the greater good. Persevere and know that, at every level, what you're doing will help us become one of the best service departments in the enterprise."

You can celebrate and reward examples of grit by employees in the organization as they happen and afterward. As another example, Jim successfully led a multiyear, multimillion-dollar modernization project. His true grit was highlighted in a weekly update, and he received a monetary bonus. "Jim," I wrote to him, "given the scope and magnitude of the mission-critical project, there were thousands of opportunities for problems and issues to arise. Your expert planning, day-to-day oversight, and proactive looking ahead resulted in an on-time and on-budget two-year implementation with no negative impacts to the enterprise. Thank you for all that you do."

Maggie was a world-class project manager. She had loads of experience, and she was smart and tenacious. She never gave up. Whenever I had a project that was going up in flames, I would call on Maggie to extinguish the fire. After she successfully saved multiple flaming projects over the years, I gave her the nickname "Red Adair," or "Red" for short. At first, she did not know if the Red Adair moniker was a compliment. After she looked him up, of course she was pleased. Red Adair was the greatest and most famous oil well firefighter: "The Adair teams completed more than 1,000 assignments internationally through the use of explosives, drilling mud, and concrete."[6] In celebration of Maggie saving yet another disastrous project, I rewarded her with a framed poster and a DVD of *Hellfighters*, the 1968 film starring John Wayne and Katharine Ross based loosely on the life of Red Adair. The poster was prominently displayed in her workspace.

Juan was yet another employee with a can-do spirit whom I entrusted to lead another risky multiyear, mission-critical project. When it was completed, he sent me this message: "I just wanted to say thanks for all your support over the years. You were the one person, through the entire transition project, that supported me and believed in me, and for that, I am truly grateful. I appreciate you giving me a chance, when not many people would."

As the leader of your organization, you must model humility and a fearless can-do will to succeed. Don't just talk about it; live it. Show that there will always be a way to move forward, even in the darkest times. Do not give in. Trust that there will always be a way to figure it out and move forward after diligently considering all the options. Remember to keep your sense of humor in even the most trying ordeals. Be sure to acknowledge, celebrate, and reward examples of true grit in your organization.

Understand their goals

Your team leaders need to know the goals and aspirations of their staff. When necessary, your team leaders need to adjust their team members' roles to be more aligned with the employees' goals and aspirations. At times, the team leaders will need your help to retain good employees. Offer to meet with those employees who are on the ledge to discuss why they want to leave the organization and to discuss alternatives.

Kathleen was an analyst who decided to leave the organization. She wanted to do something new. She and I discussed her prior work experience as a teacher, and she said that she loved teaching. Fortunately, we had an internal education program that needed a new manager. I said, "Kathleen, thanks for the open and honest conversation about your career aspirations. I understand your desire to do something new and am confident you and your team leader can create a challenging, big, impactful role that better aligns with your passion and skills in education and interest in helping us revitalize the training program."

She replied, "I've spent some time this weekend thinking about the possibility of leading the education program and agree that it is an opportunity I cannot pass up. I am very excited to be given the chance to work in a position that matches so well with my passion and experience." Kathleen successfully led the internal education program for several years.

Ken was an excellent engineer who received a lucrative offer from a local start-up. He was given only 24 hours to accept the offer, a typical recruiter pressure tactic. The company offered him more money, free drinks, snacks, lunch, dinner, massages, and dry cleaning service. His team leader and I explained that they would feed him because they expect him to work around the clock. We offered more money and promised a more balanced lifestyle to no avail. We wished him well and said, "Well, we don't say this to everyone who leaves, but if you find that you don't like it there, you are always welcome back."

After two chaotic weeks at the start-up, Ken sent this message to his team leader: "As you know, I recently started a new job. To be honest, the position and work environment aren't what I expected. The position seemed appealing and offered what I needed to take care of my family, but in the end, I feel the decision was mistakenly made. Will you take me back?" We gladly rehired Ken, and he gave us a long-term commitment to stay.

Sometimes it is too late to do anything. A talented senior consultant at the firm met with me to say she had accepted a job offer at another company in Dallas because she wanted to move there. "Why didn't you come to me before you took the new job? The firm has thousands of people and hundreds of job openings in the Dallas office. We could have transferred you there in a heartbeat." I wished her well. The lesson learned was that it is important for you and your direct reports to let all staff know that they have many other career options in the organization and that it is always safe for them to ask to discuss these options.

When necessary, work with your team leaders to adjust roles to be more aligned with their employees' goals and aspirations. At times, the team leaders will need your help to retain good employees. Offer to meet with the employee to discuss why they want to leave the organization and to brainstorm options.

Ask them to build relationships

Encourage your staff at all levels to get out of the office to let their customers know that they care. When your employees see you and your team leaders creating and building authentic business relationships with your customers, they will have effective role models to follow. Feedback from these relationships can be used to improve operations. The staff will find that, as they move up the career ladder, many of their customers are also doing so.

There was a respected peer executive of mine, James, who did not trust the wounded organization that I inherited. He was critical of the organization based on years of inconsistent service delivery and random, unsupported billings presented by the organization. I asked one of my talented team leaders, Maria, to become friends with James's trusted direct report, Elizabeth. At first Maria thought I was crazy, because "James is an arse." Nonetheless, over time through continued dialogue and improvements in our organization's service delivery and culture, Maria built a trusting and authentic professional relationship with Elizabeth, which became the key to winning the full support of James.

Early in my career at the firm, I worked with Denise, who was a client peer. She and I worked successfully on an important, highly visible project. As she moved up in her organization and I moved up in the firm, we continued to periodically get together to discuss her business challenges. Over the years, we built trust and she was comfortable reaching out to discuss problems and opportunities. We worked on two subsequent engagements that were also successful. Ten years later, Denise called me out of the blue. She was interviewing someone for a key leadership position who had worked in my department. I was happy to share my thoughts. About another 10 years later, she again called me out of the blue and said that her son was applying for an attorney position in my enterprise. She asked if her son could talk with me. "Of course!" It was just like old times. We reminisced about her son, who I first met in her office when he was five years old, and we laughed. Her son and I had a fruitful conversation, and he got the job. You know you have an authentic professional relationship when you reconnect and you pick up right where you left off—there is no time gap. When you have trusted and enduring business relationships, it is a joy to help each other whenever called on.

Authentic business relationships start at the beginning of your career and will deepen over the years. The customers you work with at all levels of your career may hire you in the future, or you may hire them. The only way to reap that later reward is to first create the authentic business relationship.

Celebrate successes

You must be intentional to change the culture of your organization. One way to do so is to communicate and celebrate success. Every six to eight weeks, my weekly blog posts would share actual customer kudos for outstanding customer service. All promotions were also celebrated in the weekly updates and in the quarterly all-staff meetings. At the conclusion of major projects, parties for staff and customers were in order: pizza, cake, doughnuts, BBQ. Here is one invitation: "For more than two years, we spent a lot of time together, meeting, planning, promoting, solving problems, and delivering the new service. Now that it's finally complete, let's come together one more time. Please join us to eat, drink, and—most of all—celebrate your tremendous accomplishment."

The fun aspect of leading an organization is that you get to show your support and directly share your gratitude to your customers and staff by participating in these joyous celebrations. During one major project, I took doughnuts to the teams working on multiple weekends. Over six months, I personally delivered 672 doughnuts. We threw a party for the customers who helped us and everyone on the project team. We invited their significant others and their children, because everyone had given up so many weekends and holidays. There was food, ice cream, and snow cones for the kids. We invited my boss, who thanked everyone for their outstanding work on a project of such great importance to the enterprise. We even had a staff jazz band, and everyone enjoyed sharing time together.

Retirements should also be communicated and celebrated: "Team, I know that most of you are aware that Helen plans to retire this Friday after 28 years of service. We will certainly miss her support and experience. We wish Helen the best as she turns this page on her life and opens a new chapter. A formal celebration will be scheduled in the upcoming weeks. We will get Helen back here to swap some stories and have a few laughs."

As the leader of the organization, you will be invited to some employees' weddings, most retirement parties, and all the funerals. Be present, and fly the flag. One time, over three weeks, we had several employees mourning the loss of loved ones, friends, and colleagues. In lieu of my weekly blog post, I sent this message: "Reflecting on this time of loss, it is difficult to focus on the tasks of daily life, including work. We support ourselves and our coworkers while continuing to serve our customers. We have all been deeply saddened by these events. I offer my heartfelt sympathies and condolences to all who have been affected. Family always comes first. I encourage you to rely on each other, as well as on your families and friends. For employees affected by the loss, the Employee Assistance Program stands ready to help. May we all find the support and comfort we need during this difficult time."

Provide transparency

Again, weekly blog posts are a great way to explain to your department and the enterprise why certain decisions have been made: "We have 12,000 laptop computers in our enterprise. Each year, about 1,200 laptops are missing, lost, or stolen, and only 30% of the 12,000 computers are encrypted. Recent high-profile worldwide data exposures have heightened our awareness of the need to take the necessary steps to secure our sensitive information. Last month, the Compliance Committee adopted a policy recommended by internal audit to encrypt all enterprise-owned laptops.

"In anticipation, last year, the leaders of the information technology organizations throughout the enterprise evaluated and selected the best encryption tool, which has been centrally funded. The central information technology organization has been working with the enterprise information technology organizations to plan and support the laptop encryption rollout by the end of December this year.

"There have been some bumps in the road, as would be expected in a population of laptop computers of our magnitude, complexity, and variety. We have documented known issues and the best practices to address these issues on the secure encryption rollout website. Those units needing more time can request an extension to the timeline by contacting the chief information security officer."

This public recap of the laptop computer encryption initiative addressing a critical internal audit finding demonstrated decision-making transparency. This transparency effectively counterbalanced critics who tried to paint this initiative as yet another half-baked idea being foisted on the enterprise by my department without doing the necessary homework. Share your decision-making thinking with all your staff and those impacted in the enterprise. This decision-making transparency builds trust.

Invest in staff development

A visible commitment to training and career development is a key responsibility when you lead an organization. In the current knowledge-driven employee marketplace, ongoing training is a given. In addition, clear career paths are necessary so employees know what is required to grow in their career.

Arthur Andersen & Co., Andersen Consulting, and Accenture have a long history of commitment to professional education and defining career paths. This deeply ingrained tradition started with Arthur Andersen himself, who was an accounting instructor at Northwestern University before opening his own firm. In subsequent decades, the firm emphasized professional education. The firm's motto was, "Think straight, talk straight."

In 1970, the firm purchased the former campus of St. Dominic College in St. Charles, Illinois, for $4 million. At the end of 1987, the Center for Professional Education in St. Charles delivered 6.8 million hours of professional education. By 1990, nearly $6,000 was invested to train each new hire. After Accenture's initial public offering in 2001, investment in employee training and development continued, reaching $411 million in fiscal year 2004. In 2005, the company started the Accenture Career Framework, which was designed to clearly articulate career progression, rewards, and training.[7]

According to *Values. Driven. Leadership: The History of Accenture*, professional education was seen as a "long-term differentiator and an important aspect of our 'best people' core value."[8] Managers and senior executives were expected to teach at least once a year, no exceptions. My last two years with the firm, I was part of a team of instructors teaching project management classes in Dublin, Ireland; Sao Paulo, Brazil; and St. Charles. The St. Charles class included 200 new managers from around the world, which was exciting.

As the leader of your organization, you and your management team must commit to helping all employees build skills. Make skills development a part of your and your management teams' interactions with all staff. Offer in-house training; third-party courses; on-demand, self-directed training, certifications, and online courses; and establish a professional education budget each year. Training budgets are best managed at the team leader level so priorities and requests can be managed at the local level, where the team leader knows exactly what their team needs.

You all have to be emotionally and materially invested in helping staff build skills and succeed. Don't be tempted to cut the training budget when funding is tight. You must continue to invest in your most important asset—your employees.

Here is an example of a weekly update committing to help all staff build cutting-edge skills: "Annual performance evaluations are due this month. I hope you all have taken time to reflect on your accomplishments and set goals for the year ahead. Consider what professional training would be most valuable for sharpening your skills and set the mutual expectation with your supervisor that you will complete this training in the coming year. All the team leaders and senior managers in our organization are committed to helping you build cutting-edge skills. Moreover, we are all committed to your career growth and a healthy work–life balance."

Throughout the year, in the weekly blog posts, we included links to relevant articles related to improving customer service, dealing with conflict, management trends, and fun topics. Often, these articles were discovered by team leaders and their team members. We would always recognize those employees who contributed to the collective organizational knowledge base. And in my office, there were multiple copies of books on hand that helped me over the years: *Managing Expectations*, *The 7 Habits of Highly Effective People*, *Crucial Conversations*, and *The Five Languages of Apology*. I would freely hand these out as discussions with employees warranted.

At times, ad hoc training is in order. After a series of painful presentations by our rising senior managers to customer steering groups, we brought in Speakeasy Inc., a communication consulting company to help the managers develop public speaking skills. Speakeasy Inc. believes effective speakers are made through the use of learnable techniques and systematic practice. We conducted several on-site courses called "Develop Your Speaking Style," which included videotaping presentations and coaching. We also encouraged staff participation in Toastmasters International. Toastmasters International offers an affordable, fun, in-person or online club environment where you can learn to present well, mentor others, and advance your career.

There are several actions that will demonstrate to all the staff in your organization that you care and are committed to their success: Demonstrate grit and model the professional will to succeed, seek to understand their career goals and aspirations even if it means staff going elsewhere, ask them to build and nurture long-term business relationships, communicate and celebrate successes and retirements, provide decision-making transparency, and invest in training and career development.

When you have the opportunity to lead an organization, build enduring professional relationships with your employees. Start by establishing the values of the organization, and create a safe work ecosystem. Let them know that you care about the well-being of them and the organization. Be emotionally and materially invested in helping all your staff to be successful.

KEY TAKEAWAYS

- Establish the values of the organization.

- Create a safe work ecosystem, especially if you inherit a wounded workgroup.

- Let them know that you care.

PART 2

The

EXTERNAL
SPHERE

of

INFLUENCE

Chapter 5

RELATIONSHIPS WITH CUSTOMERS

CREATE AND NURTURE WORKING RELATIONSHIPS WITH CUSTOMERS by seeking to understand their goals and aspirations, delivering value, and genuinely caring about their success. This will build trust and brand loyalty.

As with any of your other stakeholders, you need to understand your customers' goals and aspirations in order to help them achieve them. Some customers are external to your organization; you may also have internal customers who rely on your services. There are three steps to getting there: First, learn what you can on your own. Customers are usually ready to share; they want you to help them, and sometimes a few simple questions will get to the heart of their problem and goals. Second, determine how you can help achieve those goals. Third, set expectations and manage them while maintaining mutual accountability. This ensures that you and your customer are working in tandem rather than at cross-purposes.

Do your homework

Before you engage with a customer or potential customer, do your homework. What are the goals of their organization? What are the pain points that keep them from achieving these goals? What is the budget for the work? When you meet with a customer or potential customer, seek to understand their goals and challenges. Discuss options, possible solutions, and alternative approaches to address their needs, which may help to shape a subsequent request for proposals.

When an external customer issues a request for proposals, they typically describe the organization, goals of the initiative, scope of work, timing, and the extent of internal resources to be devoted to the project.

In the public sector, there may be funding information in annual operating or capital budgets. There also may be legislative appropriation bills describing the goals and scope of a project.

When you submit a proposal to an external customer, it must convey your understanding of the work and demonstrate that you know their organization. No boilerplate text should be used. Explain the proposed approach and how your staff will work with their internal resources to be successful.

After the firm had successfully assisted a client implement a major mission-critical program, the agency issued a request for proposals for a new financial management system. The firm had a strong track record of implementing the same financial management software in several state agencies. We proposed a highly qualified team who worked on these successful implementations. At the debriefing meeting, after we were selected, the client said that we had the best understanding of their needs, the most qualified team, a clear explanation of how we would mesh with their internal staff, and competitive pricing. We hit all the crucial points and made it clear that we were focused on their needs and not just providing a generic proposal.

At the end of the engagement, the client's executive sponsor sent this note: "Thank you for assembling such a highly qualified team of consultants to assist with this on-time and under-budget implementation and for providing valuable ongoing guidance to assure the project stayed on target. I am pleased to say that the assistance we contracted for was a very cost-effective use of the state's dollars. I enjoyed the opportunity to work with you all and thank you for your service."

Seek clarification

In addition to the information in requests for proposals, there is usually a bidder's conference where you can ask questions. Ask for clarification when needed. In addition, after the bidder's conference, there is usually a period of time to submit written questions. Take advantage of these opportunities to better understand the client's goals and aspirations. Ask, "What does success look like?" And then focus your efforts on customizing your proposal to achieve success in the way the client sees it.

Determine how you can help

Building understanding, rapport, and professional relationships with external and internal customers is critical. Asking good questions and listening are the keys to good communication and gaining a deeper understanding of customer goals and how to best realize these goals. Set accurate expectations, create a realistic project plan, and deliver the right solution on time and on budget. Even better, deliver early and under budget. You can do this in a number of ways—by scoping the work correctly, estimating the amount of effort needed, assigning the right staff, and adding sufficient schedule and budget contingencies. Actively listen to your customers, effectively respond to their needs, and meet your obligations. Over time, customers will gain confidence in your ability to deliver what you committed to do. You are a success when your customers are successful.

Set expectations and ensure mutual accountability

Your proposal is the best place to document expectations for you and your customer. Defining the scope of work, describing the approach to do the work, and conveying the staffing levels are the foundation for a healthy business relationship. Assumptions should be spelled out to reduce ambiguities. Weekly status reports should track progress and identify any open issues and their subsequent resolution. Both you and the customer need to establish mutual accountability for achieving goals.

When you are serving external or internal customers, a service-level agreement is an effective tool to set expectations. Monthly or quarterly SLA reporting establishes accountability. An SLA documents the understanding between the entity providing a service (you and your team) and the customer receiving the benefits of the service. SLAs provide transparency to service expectations and can be used between a vendor and customers or between departments in the same enterprise. SLAs will change over time, so a clear framework is needed for updating the agreements, and they should all be reviewed annually. The benefits are ensuring that everyone involved is literally on the same page, setting and managing expectations, establishing clear metrics to measure the effectiveness of the service, and offering a recourse should one of the parties fail to meet the standards outlined in the agreement. SLAs and reporting metrics establish mutual accountability and trust.

One department offered 150 services in an enterprise; however, only 10% of these services had SLAs. There was little trust between the organization providing services and the internal customers. Imagine a world where your customers have no idea what to expect for 135 services. As a service provider, you must establish your service-level metrics and create agreements with your customers; otherwise, managing customer expectations will be impossible, and mistrust will fester and grow. Some organizations also create operating-level agreements, or OLAs. These OLAs describe how an organization's internal teams will work together to achieve the service-level commitments.

Sometimes, the customer has to rely on other parts of their organization that they do not directly control to make progress. For example, some departments may be reluctant to send their staff to training for a new human resources system. One time, a department head complained that his staff did not know how to use the new human resources system. Guess what? He did not send his staff to the necessary training. Bringing this gaffe to light embarrassed the department head, who quickly sent his staff to the required training classes. In this case, a more helpful approach to ensure mutual accountability would have been to widely publish the training attendance progress by each department to highlight which departments were on-target and which were falling behind. Sharing this information with executive leadership creates peer pressure for all department leaders to stay on track. I'm a big believer in the use of peer pressure to ensure mutual accountability. Basically, you leverage public shaming to motivate department leaders who do not report to you to meet their obligations to the enterprise.

It will not be sugarplums, unicorns, and rainbows

You should also set the expectation that all will not be sugarplums, unicorns, and rainbows when transforming business processes or implementing a new system. For example, project charters to implement significant organizational change should include a section describing the Valley of Despair, which is the decline in performance when an organization goes through the process of major transition. The term comes from charts that track productivity. The line initially declines, and then, over time, productivity improves to exceed the condition prior to the major change. Wendy, a client, once asked me, "Are we now in the Valley of Despair?" My response was, "Yes, but the good news is that we will climb out of it once everyone is more comfortable with the change." And we did.

There are times when you make a recommendation and your customer or a potential customer decides not to act on it. Based on years of experience, you anticipate things will blow up in the future, but there is nothing you can do except wait. This type of decision-making is called "rolling the grenade." In your mind, you see the metaphorical grenade slowly rolling toward them, and then after you hear the "KABOOM," they are more willing to listen to you.

One client, Sharon, said that she could not afford to retain the firm to implement a new payroll system. She wanted to retain contract programmers because they would be cheaper. I cautioned that, although their hourly rate would be lower, they would not bring the project management expertise and experience to help her be successful. Fast-forward nine months. The payroll system implementation was late, and the interface to the accounting system did not work correctly. After this happened, she called for our help.

I asked, "Why did you not just call us in the first place?"

Sharon's reply was, "We needed to burn our fingers on the stove first."

Flustered, all I could say was, "Why? For the love of God, why?"

At the end of the engagement, Sharon said that she and her staff really valued the professional relationships with my consultants and that "our team's chemistry was a once-in-a-lifetime thing."

Another rolling-the-grenade example was a client executive who did not want to move her staff to a shared workspace with my team. Her staff was located on the third floor, and my team was officed on the 11th. This building literally had the slowest set of elevators on the planet. You had to schedule 20 minutes on your calendar for an elevator ride (one way). I pleaded with her to let us work together in one space to facilitate better communication. No, she did not want to ask her staff to move.

Her staff was testing the new payroll system, and my team provided technical support and fixes. The first week or two, her staff would email my team with perceived problems. It would usually take a day for them to send the issue and for my team to log the item for resolution. Then, a day or two later, a response would be sent back to her team. Sometimes, the problems were simply not knowing how to navigate the new system, and other times, fixes were needed. Well, by the third week, tensions were running high between both groups. Her staff was frustrated by how long it took to get a simple answer, and my staff was flummoxed that they were not collocated so they could solve perceived problems on the spot.

Her staff's frustration finally exploded: "KABOOM!" Now, the client executive agreed to move her staff to the 11th floor so we could all sit together. The results were magical. When issues would arise, her staff could just lean over and ask someone nearby what they thought. Hundreds of nonissues were resolved through the normal course of daily interactions. And actual problems were logged because they did need to be fixed. The morale of both groups improved dramatically, and the project's progress lurched forward.

She also had a beat-the-vendor policy directive from her executive leaders. My client was rewarded by her supervisor when she extracted free services from vendors. So, each week, my client counterpart would ask for free stuff. Often, she would try to guilt me into providing additional services at no cost by saying, "A firm like yours should have known that we would need this scope of work."

I replied, "Well, we did recognize the need; however, you did not ask for it in your request for proposals. If we had added this scope of work beyond your request, our bid would have been higher than the others, and we wouldn't have been selected. I'll be more than happy to develop a change order." We repeated these Kabuki theatrics throughout the engagement. Given that they were such a pain to work with, we doubled the budget contingency in the change orders from 15% to 30%, and she understood why.

She would also yell at me when things went wrong. Once, the response time for a new payroll system function took more than two minutes from the time you pressed the "enter" key to when the response was displayed. After she stopped yelling at me, I said we would look into it. One of my technical experts found that a switch was incorrectly set. When the switch was reset, the response time was under a second. It was a simple fix, and there was no call for yelling, but you will eventually have a customer like this. So be ready: Stay calm and fix the problems.

Later, we compared every item on 3,400 earning statements from the old payroll system with every item on the 3,400 earning statements generated by the new payroll system. We had hundreds of discrepancies on the first test. The client was furious: "There are too many &*%#@ problems!"

I tried to calmly respond, "We will investigate and explain every single discrepancy."

The first group of discrepancies related to how the data was converted. After we fixed the conversion data, half of the discrepancies went away. Second, we resolved a large number of discrepancies by adjusting the software settings. For example, one employee had 12 child support deductions, but the maximum child support deduction setting was at 10. After we increased the number of deductions allowed to a maximum of 15, the problem was resolved. Next, there was a discrepancy due to a different interpretation of a tax rule that was allowable and explainable. Finally, we found that one problem was due to the old payroll system, which had made an erroneous calculation. I made a deal with her: Please stop yelling at me when things go wrong, and I'll fix the problems.

At the end of this 18-month project, my team of 11 consultants got up to leave the project site, and not one person on the client's team said good-bye. Later, I said to her, "I'll never work for your agency again."

She laughed and said, "I don't blame you!"

Sometimes it is better to not serve a customer, especially when their expectations are unreasonable. One time I met with an executive at a major regional transit authority who wanted a new payroll system implemented in 90 days.

I said, "Honestly, it can't be done."

His face grew beet red, and he threw me out of his office. He hired another company who promised to meet the unrealistic 90-day time frame. After the implementation was six months late, the executive and the firm he hired were dismissed. I was glad he was not my customer.

At times you have to fire a customer. At one large enterprise, my team was often retained by several departments to provide various services. We developed SLAs to set expectations for the levels of service. However, we had a unique situation where we experimented with a hybrid approach of having a local customer support staff coordinate with our team. This wasn't a win–win. The person in the department would step in, cause problems, and then point the finger at us.

After several occurrences, I invited the department head, a

peer of mine, to lunch. After describing what had been happening, she said, "You're firing me as a customer, aren't you?"

I replied, "Yes, I am" and explained to her (and later explained to my team) that we did not have to provide services to everyone, especially if they are a pain. I did buy her lunch, and we did not charge them anything since the arrangement did not work out.

Finally, internal teams count on each other to provide top-quality service and meet their commitments to external customers. If one internal team misses a date, other internal teams are usually affected. Internal teams must respect and support each other with the same spirit we have for external customers. Operating-level agreements should be used to set and manage these commitments.

DELIVER VALUE

Successful customer relationships are based on delivering value. Specifically, you should always deliver something of greater value than the cost of your service.

In the early 1990s, the firm was retained by a university system to develop a reporting package for the board of regents. Key performance indicators were identified for the following strategic decision-making areas: financial management, human resources, investments, student information, research, and space utilization. The reporting package provided multiyear aggregated data and metrics for each of the nine academic and four medical campuses.

When we presented the space utilization data for each campus, a regent who had founded a nationwide hotel chain zeroed in on one campus. He noticed that the space utilization averaged only 20% from eight a.m. to five p.m. and 85% from six p.m. to nine p.m. He knew this academic campus had opened in 1975 for juniors, seniors, and a small number of graduate students who primarily attended night classes. The campus had only recently started accepting a handful of freshmen and sophomores. He saw an opportunity to maximize the use of the campus physical assets and forcefully advocated for more undergraduate classes during the day. All the other regents quickly understood that they could serve many more students with minor adjustments to the physical plant. The board of regents voted to expand the freshman and sophomore student enrollments. In 1990, the campus had a total of 8,600 students; by 2023, the campus enrollment was 31,000 students. That dramatic increase in attendance meant serving more students and a huge increase in monetary value for our client.

An executive director of a large state retirement agency retained the firm to review the operations prior to his retirement so he could provide a clear, evidence-based improvement road map for the incoming leader. An employee in the investment department recommended a better approach to improve managing cash, but the CFO refused to listen.

We learned that a $17.5-million-dollar payment was due once a month to the health insurance provider for all state employees. The agency's practice was to withdraw the funds on the first day of each month from a high-interest-bearing account and hold it in a zero-interest-bearing account, even though payment was not due until the third week of the month. We recommended an electronic funds transfer from the high-interest-rate account directly to the health insurance provider's account on the due date each month. Given the double-digit interest rate at the time, the benefits were clear.

Later, the CFO stopped me in the hall and said, "I was wondering if you would find this."

Dismayed, I replied, "You would have saved us all a lot of time and money if you had shared your ideas."

His response was, "I wanted to see how good you were."

Fortunately, the executive director implemented this one cash-management recommendation before he retired, which generated significant new interest earnings for the agency.

Sometimes you can incentivize a customer to transition to a more cost-effective service by paying for the transition. For example, we funded a $15,000, one-time transition to a new service for a client, which saved our organization $40,000 a year later. The argument for not doing it, "It's too costly to move," disappears when you pay for it. By paying for the transition, we proved our worth to the customer and ensured their happiness, and we also ended up saving actual cash. Providing value led to more value.

Success breeds success

My best customers appreciated the value of the services provided. We trusted each other and collaborated to create solutions. We worked together to plan the work and work the plan. We both made sure we had the right skilled staff at the right time. We acted as one team wearing one jersey. Together, we celebrated successes and jumped in to resolve inevitable problems. We all understood the importance of the work for the success of both of our organizations.

When you are a customer, be good to your service provider. You will get better service, more value, and higher quality by being a good customer.

In the same way providing value to customers led to more value for the firm, success bred further success. The firm has a high percentage of repeat customers because everyone enjoys mutually beneficial business relationships built on trust, where both parties are helping each other achieve success and when both are taking appropriate risks. An environment of open communication fosters collaboration. Genuine appreciation and caring for each other builds a strong foundation of trust. The quality of these business relationships directly correlates to the quality of the work, accountability, and the ability to succeed. After one success, the next challenge is easier to take on together. Of course, one still has to be competitive on pricing. Competitive pricing coupled with a proven track record of successfully working together usually wins the day.

There are tangible benefits from nurturing repeat customer relationships. According to "Helping Clients Succeed: Business Development Strategy and Skills" by Franklin Covey Company, "It costs six times more to sell to a new customer than to sell to an existing one. The odds of selling a service to a new customer are 15% and to an existing customer, 50%."[1]

Enlist support and collaboration

Customer success is fostered by enlisting support and collaboration. A great example of this is a statewide electronic medical records project that was completed six months early and under budget thanks to the support and collaboration of our client.

We have all heard about runaway IT projects and all the reasons things go bad. In Edward Yourdon's outstanding book *Death March*, he says that data and metrics suggest that "the average project is likely to be 6 to 12 months behind schedule and 50% to 100% over budget."[2] But this is not inevitable.

We worked with a state government human services agency to implement an electronic medical records system for all inpatient facilities. These facilities used paper-based medical records and had no computers. We had a realistic work plan and schedule based on two similar statewide, public-sector electronic medical records implementations. Budget and schedule contingencies were factored in. The software we deployed had a proven track record. The client's and the firm's executives were supportive and remained engaged throughout. The team had a talented senior manager, Liz, who maintained tight control of the plans and schedules, and she expertly guided the team. Team members from the state agency and the firm had a perfect balance of healthcare, state government, change management, and electronic medical records skills and experience.

The real secret of our success came from the medical records directors from every facility who actively participated in the design, testing, and development of procedures and training at the pilot institution. After the smooth go-live at the pilot facility, these leaders all said that they did not want to wait their turn. They were all ready to deploy at their facilities and asked us to accelerate the rollout across the state. Executive leadership enthusiastically embraced the new schedule, and we successfully finished six months early and under budget. No death march required.

When developing a strategy for a major university system, a high-priority initiative was "to develop the technical and applications infrastructure to support distance education" for all 13 campuses. The first draft erroneously used the term *distance learning*. After the review draft was sent to all the campuses, I received a scathing call from Dana, an international expert who said that "the correct term is *distance education*, not *distance learning*!" She had a doctorate in curriculum and instructional technology from the system's flagship university. As she was chewing me out, I had to move the phone six inches away from my good ear. When Dana finally stopped and took a breath, I asked her to meet with me to rewrite the proposed initiative. We sat shoulder to shoulder and completely rewrote it.

This initiative was approved by the board of regents, and a year later, Dana was recruited to be the first director of the newly formed distance education unit serving the system. Two years later, the firm was selected through a competitive bid process to develop a "second generation plan for distance education." We put forth recommendations for a growing organizational structure and provided a market assessment to target the degree programs and courses to be delivered. The business plan provided a sound basis for growth from that point forward.

After the second generation plan was complete, Dana said, "As always, it was a pleasure to work with you and your team. My staff found all of you to be responsive, informed, and cooperative." In the subsequent years, thousands of students took advantage of this distance education capability. Many undergraduate and graduate degree programs were now accessible in underserved areas throughout the state.

In each of these cases, the firm's success—and that of our customers—entirely depended on us working together. It was crucial to support the needs and collaborate with the customer, and it led to success beyond anything we could have achieved alone.

Request feedback

We discussed earlier that my entire management team is asked to liaise with customers every six to eight weeks. The purpose of a liaison program is to understand how well your organization is delivering services, discuss their priorities, and determine whether you can help them address their unmet business needs. Issues can be addressed quickly, which builds trust and adds to your organization's emotional bank accounts.

Another approach when supporting customers in an enterprise is to establish customer steering groups to better understand the effectiveness of your services, provide input on future improvements, and establish accountability for achieving (or not) the agreed service levels. Checking in quarterly with your customers builds trust and professional relationships that you can rely on when services are disrupted. In my first data center customer steering group meeting, one of the largest departments in the enterprise informed me that their servers had been offline for half a day. My data center staff had not told me about this outage. With egg on my face, I apologized and said that I would get to the bottom of this issue and make necessary corrections. On further investigation, an electrician had been working in the old data center and flipped the wrong breaker, which had not been properly labeled.

We immediately worked to establish consistent escalation and communication procedures for all outages. Customers and staff received timely and consistent information on unplanned and planned outages. With consistent incident reporting procedures, we were able to find patterns and strategically think of proactive ways to improve service delivery.

My weekly updates went out to hundreds of customers throughout the enterprise to keep them in the loop on major decisions and project progress. Often, they would give me unsolicited positive and negative feedback, which was always welcome. You have the potential to build your customers into your advocates. For example, after the transition to the new data center, a key member of the customer steering group sent this message: "The data center move team and all of those involved from your organization have done an amazing job. Most folks in the enterprise will never really appreciate all the skill, time, and effort that went into this amazing success."

Customer surveys are another way to glean customer feedback. Here is one comment received via a customer survey: "I couldn't be more pleased with the speed and quality of the service I've received over the past couple of weeks during an incredibly complicated and difficult transition."

Sometimes you can ask for complaints. At one large enterprise, cell phone coverage varied widely. We encouraged everyone to share their cell coverage experience—especially the bad and the ugly. By soliciting feedback via an online complaint form, we gathered all the hard evidence needed to convince multiple wireless carriers to invest in order to improve their customers' cellular experience.

Apologize when you should

As a consulting manager in an era before mobile phones, I arrived one morning at my client's office building and noticed that the glass front door had been shattered and was boarded up. I was immediately summoned to meet with the executive director, who said that one of my young consultants who had been working late the night before had kicked the door to get the attention of his coworkers and broke the glass. Bewildered and embarrassed, I said that I was very sorry, accepted responsibility, assured her that this would not happen again, and silently handed her my credit card.

Right after taking over an organization, I intercepted a draft email about to be sent to a set of customers who were using a service. The announcement was, "We have decided that the service you have been using will no longer be supported. The service will still be available, but you will use it on your own with no future bug fixes or security patches." Someone in my organization correctly decided that the service was not providing enough unique capabilities to justify the cost of improving and maintaining it, however we did not communicate the change with all of the departments using the long-standing service.

My team lead met with some—but not all—customers to get their feedback: "There were a few departments in the room, but I unfortunately didn't get everybody's name." Unfortunately, we did not have a transition path for all the customers, nor did we consult with everyone using the service; we just told them. So, we sent our apologies to all the customers of the service saying that we would not pull the plug yet. We promised to meet with each of them and walk through a transition plan and schedule. We also established a new process for retiring services that included customer participation to develop the best approaches and timing.

In addition, the outage incident-reporting procedure we established resulted in timely and consistent reporting to our customers. These reports offered transparency and became an important part of our organization's culture: openly acknowledging failures, saying we were sorry, accepting responsibility, and committing to making improvements in public and in writing because you cannot meet with all the customers impacted. The discipline of always providing outage incident reports also garnered a lot more customer appreciation of the challenges we faced.

Sometimes an apology is not necessary. One email from a professor had the subject line "Incompetence." He said, "Why are you so brain dead that the email system sends mass mailings with everybody's email address spelled out, so that when people use Reply All (which they often do), the responses go out to the whole mailing list?" In this situation, no apology was necessary. I simply asked the professor to stop using "Reply All," which solved his problem.

These skills—offering solutions, enlisting support and collaboration, requesting feedback, and apologizing when necessary—are part of delivering value for your customers. Delivering value, especially when it goes beyond what your customer pays, makes the customer feel appreciated and well served, and helps them see they've made the right choice in hiring you.

GENUINELY CARE ABOUT THEIR SUCCESS

As with your internal customers—your boss, executive leadership, direct reports, and staff—you can only support your customers fully if you genuinely care about their success. And the steps are the same as with those other groups. You should always demonstrate grit and the will to succeed and be sensitive to chemistry and timing. You should be honest if you cannot help so they can find someone who can. These elements show your clients that you are a collaborator and partner.

Dogfooding!

One method to demonstrate grit and the will to make your customers successful is called *dogfooding*. Dogfooding is trying a service internally prior to deploying to your customers. Google coined this term, derived from "eating your own dog food." Dogfooding is trying a new service to better understand how it works from your customer's point of view. This is different from testing to weed out errors, although there is a good chance you will find bugs and make fixes to improve the service. By using the service in the real world, you can better understand how to best implement the service and how to smooth the transition for your customers.

Dogfooding a new service is mandatory but not foolproof. One new enterprise service was rolled out internally to about 330 staff in my department. However, we did not test-drive the service experience long enough to truly appreciate the differences in the patchwork of personal computing technologies throughout the enterprise. Even worse, we did not take the time to exhaustively document the problems and secure resolution before starting to implement the service to our real, external customers. We also did not expect the global company supporting the service to have half-day outages and major bugs. One glaring bug was that some customer calendars were off by six hours because the company set the service on Greenwich Mean Time. This would not be fixed for 12 weeks. When we learned that some of our real customers could not do their work, we halted implementation for one year until all the 40-plus issues were resolved. Moving too quickly through dogfooding eroded customer trust, created major withdrawals from a multitude of emotional bank accounts built up over many years, and gave our department a painful metaphorical black eye.

We admitted to our customers that things had not gone as planned, apologized, and worked with our vendor and customers, which got us in a better place to successfully complete the implementation without further incident. Fortunately, this major setback did not overshadow all of our other accomplishments.

You know there will be problems. How you respond to these challenges is critical and how you will be measured. You just need to work your way through them with grit and humility. Demonstrate the will to make your customers successful by putting yourself in their shoes. Dogfooding is a useful technique to better understand how a new service will work in the real world. Just don't rush through it.

Be sensitive to chemistry and timing

A large electric utility company evaluated the chemistry between potential consulting firms and their internal team members by asking us all to cook and eat a meal together in their massive test kitchen. We were all given bright red aprons with the black embossed company logo. I thought this was a great way to evaluate how well people worked together and to determine whether we bonded when breaking bread. Unfortunately, we were not selected, but I still have my red apron as a fond souvenir.

The chemistry with your customers or potential customers can change over time. One time, I was proposed to be one of the team leaders on a transformation program at a large university. At the oral presentation of our proposal, I fervently spoke about how we would work together during the multiyear project. We, the proposed team leaders, met with customer executives and senior members of the faculty over lunch and discussed the importance of the program. After I returned to the Austin office, my managing partner called me to say that the firm was selected but the customer did not want me to be a team lead because I was "short and abrupt." Yes, this news bruised my ego, but hey, there would be no commuting halfway across the country each week for the next couple of years. I found out later that they even gave me a nickname: "The Preacher."

Fast-forward a year and a half. The transformation program was now in trouble, and my boss sent me there to interview for the overall program leader position. The customer asked me to come on board and we successfully completed the multiyear program. So, at a later time they actually did need someone who had the faith and enthusiasm of a preacher and who could be short and abrupt when necessary.

Be sensitive to chemistry and timing with your customers. They may not think you are a good fit at first, but you may be asked to help at a later time when conditions change.

Be honest if you cannot help

A large community college selected the firm for a major project. Unfortunately, the contract sat on their attorney's desk for nine months. By the time their attorney finalized the contract, the seasoned team of consultants that we proposed was working on other engagements. I was honest with the customer and said we could not do the work because the experienced team we proposed was no longer available and gave him a list of qualified firms who could help them. He appreciated my honesty.

Genuinely care about your customer's success. Demonstrate grit and the will to succeed, be sensitive to chemistry and timing, and be honest if you cannot help and find someone who can. Build mutually beneficial business relationships with customers by seeking to understand their goals and aspirations, delivering value, and genuinely caring about their success. You will be successful when your customers are successful.

KEY TAKEAWAYS

- Seek to understand the goals and aspirations of your customer.

- Deliver value.

- Genuinely care about your customer's success.

Chapter 6

RELATIONSHIPS WITH PEERS AND INFLUENCERS

WHETHER YOU ARE WORKING IN YOUR OWN enterprise or providing services to an external customer, you need to know who your peers and influencers are. Peers are at the same level that you are in an organization. Influencers can be at any level in an organization. Once you identify who they are, you need to understand how you can help each other. You need to seek to understand the values, goals, and aspirations of your peers and influencers; enlist support and collaborate; and demonstrate that you genuinely care about their success.

UNDERSTAND THEIR VALUES AND GOALS

To determine who your peers and influencers are, you'll need to first find out who has the power. Who is the person other people listen to? Who drives decisions? Who else do you need to be talking to? Once you identify them, ask how you can help each other. Finally, set and manage expectations and mutual accountability, just like you would in any other business relationship.

Who has the power?

If you want to have a positive impact as a changemaker in an organization, you need to identify the most powerful people. Start with the organization chart, and create a power map. Power mapping is a technique to visualize the most powerful and influential people. On the organization chart, circle the CEO and the executive team. Then look within each organizational area to identify peers and influencers.

Michael Boyles wrote "Power Mapping: What It Is & How to Use It" for the Harvard Business School Online's *Business Insights* blog. He said that you need to identify central individuals "within a network who are the main source of information and advice. They don't necessarily hold the greatest authority or [the] most impressive job titles but have significant influence because of their control over company information."[1]

Once you identify the central people, you need to understand what they value. They may value tangible resources, such as space in buildings, or intangible qualities, such as experience, safety, status, and affiliation. Boyles says the two most common mistakes when building a power map are omission and commission: "Omission [is] neglecting to identify individuals who are as powerful when they're central and highly influential. Commission [is] assuming people are more powerful and influential than they actually are."[2]

In one large enterprise, the chief of staff for the CFO was a central individual. She had worked in the enterprise for more than 25 years and had the complete confidence of the CFO. She built a vast network throughout the enterprise that would help her and the CFO solve significant issues relating to the allocation of financial resources. In a similar enterprise, the chief of staff for the CFO was relatively new to the organization and mostly worked on one-off projects. When I met with her to understand what she valued, she actually said that she was not very influential and advised me to not waste my time meeting with her. Great advice!

Ask what they value

After you have completed the power mapping, you and your direct reports should meet with these central individuals. Extending the liaison program to peers and influencers in your enterprise provides an opportunity to directly show support and ask what they value. These ongoing dialogues create a better understanding of how their business needs change over time.

A peer of mine, Ellen, was responsible for transforming undergraduate education. I reached out to her to understand how my organization could better support her program. Ellen needed a better learning management system to support new approaches that would revolutionize the delivery of the curriculum. She became an executive sponsor on a project to replace the old, buggy, and clunky learning management system. We created a faculty- and student-led evaluation and selection process, which became a model for subsequent large-scale change initiatives. We pooled staff from both of our organizations to support the two-year transition. Support contacts were recruited in all the departments in the schools and colleges.

At the end of the transition, the support contacts sent a letter to the president that said, "We, the undersigned, represent the vanguard of one of the largest projects ever undertaken by the university. While 'changing learning management systems' sounds like an obscure IT project, the fact of the matter is that it affects 52,000 students and 4,000 faculty members. As we mark the end of this two-year transition, we want to take this opportunity to acknowledge a job well done."

Both of our organizations were inclusive and available, communicated often, advocated on behalf of the campus, and provided subject matter expertise. Inclusion brought all the support contacts in the departments together frequently, where we listened with patience and respect and implemented the best solutions possible. The combined team was always available to assist the support contacts, and they "were always treated with respect." One support contact said in the email to the president, "Not just respect though, downright friendliness and genuine humor, an atmosphere of camaraderie that always felt like a joint effort amongst us all."

There were multiple paths of communication. The combined team became tireless advocates for the faculty and students with the vendor, and we were able to secure many positive outcomes and enhancements from the vendor. The combined team focused on solutions to disparate problems and effectively connected people with problems to subject-matter experts with solutions.

After you identify the peers and influencers through power mapping, ask them what they value, and share what you value. Find areas where you can help each other address business needs, and continue this dialogue via a formal liaison program.

How can you help each other?

Here are two examples of peers helping each other.

A peer of mine needed space in a building that my department managed. He asked me for about 1,500 square feet of office space for a new high-priority unit he was establishing. When we were discussing his needs, he mentioned that he had a relatively new Chevrolet Suburban that was not being used. My organization always needed to replenish our fleet of 100 vehicles, so we traded the 1,500 feet of office space and a classroom in my building for the Suburban.

Another peer, David, was a genius at the firm. We worked together to turn around that troubled $100 million project discussed earlier. We reestimated the remaining work to establish realistic budgets and schedule. Then he led the technology team, and I became responsible for the application development team. Often, we would collaborate to solve knotty problems.

Being supersmart, David would go from the beginning of solution A to answer Z in nanoseconds. He always leaped to an answer: "It's Z!" I am more of a plodder and would slow him down and walk us both through each step of the way toward a solution. This drove him absolutely insane. Often, we would find that steps were missing. By the end of the discussion, we would come up with a workable approach by helping each other. Together, we were better than either of us was alone.

Expectations and mutual accountability

It is important to set expectations with your peers and influencers and to hold each other accountable. Elect to see the good in everyone. Unfortunately, there are times when a peer is a bully, a narcissist, or a manipulator with an overall disregard for others. Here is an example of how to deal with an unprofessional peer.

Frank was the most challenging peer that I ever worked with. Most of my peers have been genuine, supportive, and generous. Many became and still are good friends. I was supportive of their initiatives, and they reciprocated.

Frank, Martha, and I reported to the same supervisor. Frank and Martha had worked for the boss for more than 10 years, and I was the new guy. Frank said that the boss wanted him to be a "watchdog"; you might remember this story from earlier.

Following the old adage "keep your friends close and your enemies closer," I met with Frank in his large, honey oak—paneled office every other week. It was odd that there were never any papers on his desk, only an open Bible. Luckily, he had an automatic espresso machine in his office, and we both appreciated the rich smell and taste of the freshly brewed shots.

Frank denigrated people. He spoke ill of Martha, me, and our direct reports. He would pretend to confide in me his negative perceptions of Martha and her team. And you knew he was doing the same with Martha—and the boss—about me and my team. This was a huge distraction from the real, difficult work at hand.

Frank aspired to be a "servant leader" but acknowledged that he had been a bad role model for Doug and Dawn, his direct reports, and that they had earned terrible reputations. Frank was the watchdog, while Doug and Dawn were his pit bulls.

Over the years, other organizations in the enterprise were targeted by the watchdog. Consequently, the open dissension Frank sowed became visible across the enterprise, which reflected badly on both the boss and Frank. After brutal feedback from some of the boss's peer colleagues, he decided Frank needed an intervention. He asked Martha and me to give Frank some feedback and coaching.

I let Frank know that I asked my direct reports to always take the high road when dealing with him, Doug, and Dawn. I said that we proactively embraced a nonviolent strategy to deal with them: "You can beat us with batons, send Doug and Dawn—your pit bulls—out to chew on us, and blast us with water cannons, but we will keep marching across the bridge and keep our eyes on the prize." Thankfully, soon after this intervention, Frank left the enterprise.

You have to wonder how the Franks, Dougs, and Dawns of the world live with themselves. Don't be like them. Villains always think they are doing the right thing, which justifies them hurting people. The classic book *The 48 Laws of Power* by Robert Greene, which I discussed earlier, is an excellent primer for the dirty tricks that are used to disorient and destabilize others while consolidating power. You need to understand these unscrupulous techniques used against you by bad people so you are in a better position to protect yourself.

I only have one regret from my long career: trusting people who shouldn't have been trusted. So, be on the lookout for these untrustworthy traits: fake niceness, no basic respect for confidentiality, no accountability, not taking responsibility for their damaging actions, spreading rumors about you to others, gossiping about others to you, lack of empathy, failure to uphold commitments, and always seeing themselves as a saint when they are often the devil.

ENLIST SUPPORT AND COLLABORATE

You can build effective business relationships with peers and influencers in the same way you have built them for your other business relationships: Start by enlisting support and collaboration, requesting feedback, and offering an apology when one is called for.

Cultivate the lines of communication

It is your responsibility to reach out to your peers and influencers to understand what their values are, to share your values, and to discover ways you can help each other. Include naysayers so you can understand their issues with your organization and seek to resolve those issues. Set meetings on a monthly, bimonthly, or quarterly basis, depending on the extent to which your departments work together. In addition, my weekly updates went out to all the peers and influencers to keep them in the loop on major decisions and project progress. Often, I would receive positive and negative feedback in return, which was always welcomed. You have the potential to turn peers and influencers into your advocates.

One peer of mine, Bill, was a true war hero. After many years of service to our country, he earned a doctorate and was put in charge of campus safety and security. I reached out to him to understand how my IT department could help in time of need.

We both realized that it would be a matter of when, not if, campus safety and security would be threatened. I let Bill know that campus safety and security was priority number one for me and my department. During my eight years at the university, we had a murder, a shooting, a bomb scare, and a widespread power outage, and we were able to work together to minimize the damage and ensure the safety of the campus during and after each incident. Foresight and cooperation are crucial even when—or maybe especially when—you're not in a crisis.

Our first order of business was to be certain that the three emergency operations centers were functioning with up-to-date network equipment, video conferencing, cable TV, and copper phone lines in case the network was not working. The primary emergency operations center was near the offices of the executive leadership team and was up to date. If that building was compromised, a second emergency operations center was across the street, in my building. That room needed a lot of work to upgrade all the technology and verify that it was working the way it should. A third emergency operations center was in Bill's building, on the far side of campus. That room was up to date. We agreed to ask our staff to test all three rooms quarterly to ensure that they would support the executive leadership team during a crisis.

Bill and I met every month to discuss what was going well and what we could do together to improve campus safety and security. For example, when my organization replaced 21,000 copper telephone lines and switched to the fiber data network for voice communications, we made sure that we had the right number of copper lines retained in the elevators, machine rooms, parking garages, and emergency call boxes. We prepared together for huge events like commencement and football games. Bill and his direct reports were invited to participate in annual emergency preparation tabletop exercises that my organization ran to practice how my team would work with his to respond to a number of disaster scenarios. Bill and I always learned afterward how to improve our organizations' responsiveness.

Bill was also very good at sharing rumors with me, which enabled us to nip them in the bud. After a four-hour power outage, the first in 10 years, Bill said that he heard a rumor that my department "did not have enough diesel fuel for the backup generators." Well, two of the generators used natural gas for fuel, so no issue there. The third generator, which did use diesel fuel, was topped off on a monthly basis and would provide approximately 24–36 hours of continuous operation. Bill let the source of the rumor know that their concern was unfounded.

In another instance, Bill sent this message: "Brad, I was in the Research Safety Committee meeting yesterday, and there was concern about whether the new employee training system has enough licenses for students. Students that work in labs are required to take compliance training, and the record of the training has to be retained." I replied, "That's a valid concern if it is true. Let me check into it and get back to you." The good news was that we did consider student employees in the number of licenses.

I would also give Bill a heads-up if there was a service outage that would impact his operation and provided regular updates until the problem was resolved.

It is your duty to reach out to your peers and influencers to enlist support and discover ways you can help each other.

Request feedback

You are not a mind reader. When you meet with your peers and influencers, ask them for feedback. In large enterprises, there are thousands of ways to miscommunicate, drop balls, and make mistakes. There are also a thousand ways to get things right. You want to hear both.

After letting a team leader go due to his mismanagement of the $32 million construction project described earlier, I reached out to meet with my peer, Katherine, who was responsible for construction and maintenance of all the buildings. She was frustrated with my department, especially with my newly departed team leader, and she was relieved that a new project director was in place.

First, I apologized for all the past bad behavior and said, "We want to be better partners." She appreciated my intent to improve the relationship between our departments. When we met, she shared the history of decision-making (or the lack thereof), and we discussed how to improve the relationship going forward. We found a number of areas where the prior project director "was supposed to talk with someone in her organization." These communications either did not happen or were poor. We agreed that better planning and communication were needed, and I pledged to be sure we included her direct reports in these efforts. Our organizations worked together to successfully complete the new facility, and as peers, we developed a strong mutually beneficial business relationship based on mutual trust.

Every time you meet with your peers and influencers, ask them for feedback. Ask them to reach out to you with good and bad news. You are not alone. Your peers and influencers are your partners; they are the ones rowing with you. They are facing similar challenges, and collaboration is essential.

Offer apologies

When you, your direct reports, or anyone in your organization screws up, apologize. It is the art of apology that counts.

Sometimes the right hand in a large organization does not know what the left hand is doing. When we proposed the installation of a new building access control system, we needed to present and gain approval from the president's cabinet and the budget council. We invited Bill to the cabinet meeting but by mistake not to the budget council meeting.

He responded to my team leader, "I did not know we were going to the budget council. I am concerned that I am being closed out."

The team leader's reply was, "I apologize. That was certainly not the intent. I knew you wanted to attend the cabinet meeting, but I did not have anything in my notes about you wanting to attend the budget council meeting and am sorry for missing that."

I also sent this note to Bill: "I am sorry we dropped the ball. We got out of sync with all the last-minute rescheduling of the cabinet meeting. I'll be more careful in the future. I hope you will forgive the lapse."

There are thousands of ways to miscommunicate and make mistakes. When you or anyone in your organization screws up, apologize.

GENUINELY CARE ABOUT THEIR SUCCESS

You're probably noticing a pattern by now. Building effective relationships with your peers and influencers requires the same focus as creating and nurturing other authentic business relationships. One crucial factor is genuinely caring about their success. To show that you do care, demonstrate grit and the will to succeed, and be sensitive to self-interest and timing.

Trying to part the Red Sea

Many of the initiatives you work on can span a number of years, so you need to show that you have the stamina to see them through. You cannot give up.

My first example relates to finding a place for a new network operating center. The old network operating center, which supported the statewide network and the local network, was situated in a decrepit and scary building located in a flood zone. The campus master plan called for razing that building in a few years. We needed to find a site nearby to reduce the cost of moving tens of thousands of fiber cables and the copper lines supporting campus safety and security. I reached out again to Katherine, the peer of mine who was responsible for construction and maintenance of all the buildings. We worked well together to successfully complete the $32 million construction project, which was in flames when I first started.

I said, "Katherine, I'm still trying to learn the design and construction process here and get ahead of the curve. I want my department to be a good citizen. Let's meet with our direct reports to discuss the business and operational needs of a new primary network operating center. I keep wandering campus like Moses in search of a new, cost-effective, and resilient home. I appreciate you helping to shepherd us out of the current slavish building."

Katherine replied, "It does feel like we are trying to part the Red Sea, and I sometimes think that I'm like the Egyptians who got caught up in Moses's wake."

Together, our organizations created the statement of need, and my department funded the preliminary design work. Two years later, a new 430,000-square-foot, $310 million building was approved for construction next door to our old building. Working with Katherine, her boss, and my supervisor, we were able to include the new primary network operating center into the design and construction of this new building. Being located nearby saved millions of dollars in the cost to move the fiber cables and copper lines. Six years later, the construction was complete. Four years after that, the new primary network operating center began operations. The scary building was demolished a couple years later.

Another example of grit relates to the annual performance appraisal and promotion process at the firm. A woman working for me, Kerri, was an outstanding performer. The clients loved her, and she really delivered with excellence. During the annual performance appraisal process one year, the firm's policy was to group staff into bands. When people were on the borderline, we were required to force a certain percentage of staff into each band: A, B, C. Kerri was force-banded into the B band, despite my advocacy that she be in the A band. The Human Resources manager assured me that being force banded would not impact future promotion decisions. Fast-forward a year, and Kerri was up for promotion. I discovered that, because she had been forced into the B band in the prior year, she was not going to be promoted. On the last day of the promotion cycle, I marched down to her career counselor's office—a peer of mine—and said, "This is not right. Let's fight for Kerri's promotion to manager."

I reminded him of the assurance from human resources that force banding would not hold someone back from promotion. We called the senior executive in Minneapolis overseeing the promotion process and stated our case for Kerri. She agreed with us and yelled out to her assistant: "Flip the switch! Flip the switch!" And Kerri was promoted to manager. We both went to the mat for Kerri, and we would not be denied.

Demonstrate that you care by showing true grit when facing daunting challenges.

Be sensitive to self-interest and timing

Although the goal is to seek win–win solutions to problems between your peer department heads and influencers, there will be times when a peer colleague or influencer will not work with you, especially if it is not in their self-interest or if the timing is not right.

A peer of mine managed the print service for the enterprise. My department had agreed long ago, before my time, to pay $100,000 per year for print services, but there was no documentation codifying this agreement. The actual printed reports were not used by my organization but by three other departments overseen by three more of my peers, who were not interested in evaluating whether the reports were still needed. None of them had any motivation to reduce this cost to my organization. Every week I would see a van unloading six boxes of printed reports and wondered if anyone used them or if they were just used to prop doors open. My department even offered a service where their staff could access the reports online. Even worse, one of the departments paid to have their printed reports scanned so they could access them online instead of using the existing online reporting service. I raised this wasteful situation to my supervisor, but two of her departments wanted the paper reports, so she did not do anything to help reduce this waste of funds.

A peer in a large department wanted to stop paying my department for his telephone service. He installed a small voice-over-Internet-protocol telephone system on the campus data network. He touted this "savings" to other peers in the enterprise. He even had a presentation entitled "Why Rent the Cow When You Can Buy the Cow?" One time, his telephone system failed. Who do you think he called to fix it? Yes, he called my technical staff for help. I explained that he was not being a good citizen, because the monthly telephone service rate he was no longer paying covered the cost of the copper telephone lines needed for safety and security in his buildings. "Do you want me to pull all the copper lines from your elevators and machine rooms?" Of course, I would never do this. He just did not care. When we moved the entire campus telephone voice service to the data network, executive leadership outlawed these rogue attempts by my peers to avoid paying their fair share.

Another peer of mine had a mission-critical system supported by a guy who moved to Vietnam. In my mind, I pictured Colonel Kurtz in the 1979 film *Apocalypse Now* sitting in front of an old desktop computer with a dial-up modem. I asked my peer colleague, "What if he gets hit by a water buffalo? What is your backup plan?" We offered to help document this system and provide a local team for ongoing support to eliminate a single point of failure. No deal.

You do not have line authority over your peer colleagues. They do not work for you, so there is not much you can do, especially if it is not in their self-interest. The only recourse is to enlist support from your supervisor, but there are times where your supervisor or an interim boss has a conflict of interest, and it will be time to retreat to fight another day.

Creating and nurturing authentic business relationships with your peers and influencers helps you navigate issues, conflicts, and setbacks. But you first need to know who your peers and influencers are. Peers are at the same level as you are in the organization. And power mapping helps you identify the key influencers who have power. You need to reach out to those peers and influencers to enlist support and collaborate.

KEY TAKEAWAYS

- Seek to understand the values, goals, and aspirations of your peers and influencers.

- Enlist support and collaborate.

- Demonstrate that you genuinely care about their success.

Chapter 7

RELATIONSHIPS WITH STRATEGIC VENDOR PARTNERS

AT THE FIRM, MY GOAL WAS TO BE a strategic vendor partner with my clients. "Vendor" implies a short transactional relationship, like you have with a vending machine. I became a strategic vendor by understanding the goals and aspirations of my customers by building the relationship beyond a transaction. When I was on the customer side of the desk, my goal was to build mutually beneficial relationships with vendors we deemed strategic. Let's focus now on the customer's point of view. You should seek to understand the goals and aspirations of your vendors, ensure that vendors deliver value, and genuinely care about your mutual success.

UNDERSTAND THE GOALS AND ASPIRATIONS OF YOUR VENDORS

The best way to build a strategic relationship with your vendors is to follow these four steps: First, identify the companies you deem strategic. This will narrow the field of contacts and relationships you need to create. Second, ask your strategic vendor partners to help you drive value. By enlisting their support to help your product or service succeed, you help the vendor be successful as well. Third, determine how you can help each other. By nurturing this relationship, you will both benefit in the long run. Finally, set and manage expectations and mutual accountability so that you are both doing what you say you'll do and will achieve success as you define it.

Identify strategic vendors

Not all of your vendors are strategic. Step back and research where you are spending the most money, and identify which companies are providing mission-critical products and services.

Like most organizations, I had my most-favored vendor list and my most-hated vendor list. Places on both lists were well earned by companies by either being responsive and caring about who we were as a customer or not. Cold sales calling is transactional and never works. In fact, I never answer my telephone when people call the number in the directory. Cold-calling sales emails sent to the CEO also never work.

Ask your strategic vendor partners to help you drive value

Ask your strategic vendor partners to help you solve business and technical problems. Ask them to bring industry knowledge regarding business trends, future technologies, and their competitors. Show them your organization's strategy and values, and ask them to share information, provide insight into future services, and offer solutions. You want them to deeply understand your goals, aspirations, and culture. You should also seek to understand their goals, aspirations, and values.

When we were nearing completion of the $32 million facility, we budgeted for network equipment. However, the current line of equipment we budgeted for was about to be superseded with a new, much more capable offering. We wanted to move up to the next generation of equipment to extend the life of this investment by several years. Our network vendor decided to deeply discount the next generation equipment to the amount we had originally budgeted for the current line of equipment so we could take advantage of the technical enhancements for many years to come. The motivation for the strategic vendor was to have our enterprise be a great reference for their new offering, which we were happy to do. Our account representative said, "I want to say thank you for your business and partnership over the years. Our business relationship has really strengthened over time, and the respectful and fair nature you demonstrated toward us was a major part of that."

Another strategic vendor partner was our learning management system provider. We were early adopters of a forward-thinking, cloud-based solution, and the company welcomed our requests for improvements to make their product more marketable. They made sure the solution was accessible and easy for faculty and students to navigate. Unlike the prior vendor, they built the product from the ground up using industry standards. This approach enabled us to securely integrate a variety of support tools and the student email system in a matter of hours.

We had never been able to securely connect the student email system with the prior vendor's product, and they did not care.

In addition, the new company was flexible when we negotiated pricing. Most companies in this marketplace price their product by the number of students and faculty. Well, any number times 52,000 students and 4,000 faculty is a big number. We proposed paying only for the students and faculty who actually used the service. We estimated how many students and faculty would use the system at the start of a semester and did a true-up with the actual numbers at the end of each semester. This pricing approach saved us hundreds of thousands of dollars over the years.

Ask your strategic vendor partners to help you solve business and technical problems. Show them your organization's strategy and values, and ask them to share information and offer solutions. You want them to understand your goals, aspirations, and culture and deeply care about your success.

Determine how you can help each other

Conduct quarterly business reviews with your strategic vendors. Review their performance in the past quarter, and discuss how to continuously improve the relationship. These meetings should be designed to be sure both parties' obligations are being met. We included our account representative and their immediate supervisor. We would also include our director of purchasing, who was a peer colleague of mine, and his team lead. We discussed what was going well with the relationship, problems, potential changes, planned projects, and current and future products.

It is also good to create relationships with senior vice presidents of sales. Often, they can help you influence their organization to resolve issues and make product improvements. The senior vice president for sales at our learning management systems company and I talked frequently as we transitioned to the new solution. He sent me an email saying, "Just checking in to ensure that things went well today. Hope you had a good one. Our guys are monitoring things closely, and we will rally the troops right away if needed." That was great customer service. The only time I heard from the prior learning management system vendor's account representative was once a year, when he wanted his annual check for maintenance.

Determine how you can help each other be successful by conducting quarterly business reviews with your strategic vendor representatives. Build relationships with the senior vice presidents of sales to help you influence the company.

Managing expectations and establishing mutual accountability

My expectations for strategic vendors are that they bring ideas to drive greater value and reduce costs, bring the best people to help us (but not too many), invest marketing funds to add value, be responsive to requests for information, anticipate problems, apologize and not blame us or others when there are problems, be transparent, and act with honesty and integrity.

One account representative pitched the idea of outsourcing all of our computing needs to her company. She described all the benefits to us. Given that she knew how much we spent annually buying computers from her company, I asked, "How much would we save?"

She gulped and said, "It will cost 20% more than what you are currently spending."

My reply was, "But we want to reduce costs, not increase them."

She countered, "But you will get more stuff with this offer."

Astounded, I said, "We don't want more stuff! We need to reduce costs!"

We discovered that she would also offer differing discounts to other departments in the enterprise, and that she made ad hoc, end-of-quarter discounts for some but not all that created ill will between departments. After months of trying to improve the relationship to no avail, I requested a new account representative.

The director of purchasing and I did successfully work with the replacement account representative to establish standard configurations for laptop and desktop computers and servers. Departments throughout the enterprise were able to take advantage of the total-volume buying power of the enterprise and the resulting cost savings. During the first year of this program, 83% of desktop purchases and 63% of laptop purchases were ordered using the standard configurations. The resulting savings that first year was approximately $250,000 more than the already discounted pricing. Next, we worked to establish discounts on all equipment based on the total annual $10 million enterprise spend, so that the first piece of equipment purchased during the year and the last purchase of the year all received the same deep discount based on the total spend.

Another strategic vendor was meeting with various departments in the enterprise to sell two different video-conferencing products, one a costly high-end system and the other a web-based lower-fidelity system. They donated one high-end system to a department, but like a free puppy, there were significant ongoing maintenance costs to keep the system operational. The bigger issue was that we already had a video-conferencing product from a different company that was centrally funded and supported. We asked them to cease and desist selling these products, which they did. We still had to support the free puppy, though.

You and your partner vendors should work together to supply your organization in a way that aligns with your goals while also meeting theirs. But you can only do that if you nurture strong business relationships with the best—most strategic—vendors and ensure accountability on both sides.

ENSURE THAT VENDORS DELIVER VALUE

It is your responsibility to ensure that vendors deliver value. Like we've discussed for every other relationship, they should always offer options to resolve problems. They should offer and solicit feedback so you can both improve the relationship. And, as always, they should expect, accept, and offer apologies when they are appropriate.

Offer options to resolve problems

You will have problems with your vendors. When those problems arise, you need to work together to find solutions to prevent an adversarial supplier relationship.

We had some mission-critical equipment that continued to fail. We reached out to the account representative, who said, "We had advised your department not to purchase this equipment for the intended use."

My team leader said, "I have plenty of emails documenting our conversations with the sales and technical representatives when we purchased the equipment. None of them mentioned any concern with their use at all. They did say the equipment would have lower performance numbers but never went so far as to say it was not appropriate."

My response to the account representative was, "Ryan, I am always concerned when a vendor blames the client for 'forcing us to sell them the wrong thing.' When I was in the vendor role, I would never sell a product to a client if I knew the product would not work, even if it meant not booking the sale."

Ryan said, "In this case, this product was ordered by your organization anyway and was set up and running by the time I found out that they had gone ahead with the order. I believe you have a very capable team that made the best decision they could with the budget they had at the time."

I escalated this issue to Ryan's supervisor's boss for resolution. She said she would "make it right, no matter who made what decision for whatever reason on either side." She did so, and we were assigned a new sales representative.

Problems are inevitable, but beware when the vendor blames you, the client, for the problem. That is a red flag. You need to work together to find options to resolve solutions, no matter who was at fault.

Offer support and collaboration

When there are major problems, you need to work with your vendor by offering support and collaboration. In order for them to do so, you'll need to give them the chance to act. That means clear communication in a timely manner and celebrating when they succeed. Being a good customer encourages good vendors to provide better service, offer more value, and deliver higher quality. Your overarching goal is to be the best customer they ever had.

We hired a company to help us implement the new telephone service over the data network. The first project manager was very capable, and the work was going extremely well. However, after she took maternity leave, her replacement project manager was difficult to work with, and the project started to fall apart. When we escalated this issue to John, the vice president responsible for sales, he pledged to be continually engaged with his team and us throughout the upcoming months until he was positive we were experiencing the same level of confidence we had six months earlier.

John said, "I met with my team to understand the complexities of this deployment and figure out the best way to overcome the hurdles, including adding the right resources where necessary. My primary goal is to collaborate with you on the best options near and long term to get this project back on track without disruption."

He came on-site to meet with his team and us for several days to personally understand the root causes of the problems, and we together came up with solutions that would benefit both of our teams. The newly assigned resources worked to resolve our issues, and a month later, the deployment was proceeding the way we expected it to go.

I sent John a note: "Just a quick update to say that the project is now heading in the right direction. I'm happy to say that we are back on track. We really like what we are seeing with Betsy and Eileen. Please continue to give them your full support."

Give your strategic vendor partners an opportunity to collaborate with you to solve problems, and give them positive feedback when they come through.

Offer and solicit feedback

Strategic vendor partners are not mind readers. Use your words. If you are unhappy, let your account representative know. If the account representative is not responsive, then raise the issue up the management chain until you get a satisfactory resolution. In addition, ask for feedback regarding your organization's work and behaviors.

We retained a global consulting firm to develop a master plan for administrative systems. I was having trouble working with the senior manager, Jack, who was assigned to lead the engagement. I initiated weekly meetings with him to try to keep the project on track. Unfortunately, he did not follow through on a number of issues, so I escalated his poor performance to the partner in charge of the engagement.

I shared my concerns with her. First, Jack aligned himself with duplicitous Frank, which reduced his credibility with other business owners. He treated Frank as the only client executive who mattered, a classic consultant mistake. I asked Jack to send me an agenda prior to our weekly checkpoint meetings, and when I received one 30 minutes before we were due to meet, I had to ask him to send me agendas the day before from that point forward. His invoices did not list the hours worked by person, nor did they itemize the out-of-pocket expenses.

I said to the partner, "You now understand why I am disappointed with your company's performance to date and very worried about the outcome. I know you realize this work needs to be conducted with excellence. It's time for you to step up and help."

Unfortunately, the client partner was no help. We limped along with Jack until we, the client team, completed the master plan. The partner fired Jack after our project, which was too late to help us. We never hired that firm again, nor did they dare ask us to be a reference.

Here are the thoughts that I shared with the partner on what makes a great consultant:

- They exceed client expectations.

- They build long-term business relationships and become a trusted advisor.

- They have a passionate desire to learn about the client's business, strategy, and objectives.

- They offer options to solve problems and recommend tailored solutions.

- They demonstrate personal integrity, initiative, empathy, and competence.

- They are patient and respectful: a humble practitioner.

- They are willing to tactfully take a stand.

- They thrive under pressure and deliver on time and on budget.

- They ask for help and apologize when necessary.

- They ask good questions and actively listen.

These are also the traits of exceptional employees.

You have to communicate clearly and completely what you do and do not appreciate about the work. If you don't ask for help, your vendor contact (or their supervisor) may have no way of knowing you are dissatisfied—and so can't fix your problem. If they fail to address your needs, it's time to move up the company's management chain until you get a satisfactory resolution—otherwise, never retain them again.

Expect, accept, and offer apologies

Things will go wrong, and everyone makes mistakes. When they do, expect, accept, and when necessary, offer an apology. The only way to move past an issue is to embrace responsibility and work together to fix it.

One global company made a mistake that caused an outage for the enterprise. Loren, our account representative, said, "I just want to apologize once again for the huge mistake and lack of oversight on our end. I appreciate you handling this entire situation so graciously (you know, once you all pulled your jaws off the floor). My boss and I will be quickly working on next steps so this does not happen again and will get back to you and Maggie as soon as possible. We really value our relationship with your organization and would like to continue to build upon it in the future, so please feel free to reach out directly to me with any issue, large or small."

My reply was, "You are most welcome, Loren. Luckily, we were sitting around a conference table, so our jaws hit the table, not the floor. Good business partners tell each other the truth and apologize when they mess up, which you did today. We appreciate that."

You get more from your strategic vendor partners with positive reinforcement (honey), than with vitriol (vinegar). However, it is your responsibility to ensure vendors deliver the value they promised. Both you, as the customer, and your strategic vendor partners should communicate clearly and openly about the service or product, including offering apologies when necessary.

GENUINELY CARE ABOUT THEIR SUCCESS

As with any other relationship, in order to ensure success, you have to genuinely care—that includes relationships with your strategic vendor partners. Your business—and the relationship they're trying to build with you—is a huge motivator. Understand the influence you have and use it. You'll also need to stay vigilant; otherwise, you'll lose sight of the goal or never know whether you've reached it. Finally, you should always demand—and provide—honesty and integrity in every partnership.

Understand your role as motivator

Having a successful strategic vendor partner will help you be more successful; they will help you solve problems, quickly address issues, and offer you better deals. You need to ask what motivates their company. You also need to work with them when there is a crisis. When you are working with a global firm, you need to escalate issues up the management chain until you find an executive—typically the senior vice president of sales—who understands the importance of both organizations being successful.

Remember the major project snafu in chapter 5, "Relationships with Customers," where a global company supporting a mission-critical service had multiple half-day outages and major bugs? One glaring bug was that some customer calendars were off by six hours because the company set the service on Greenwich Mean Time, a problem that would not be fixed for at least 12 weeks.

We also made some serious mistakes; we stopped our internal dogfooding too early. We should not have started migrations until all the open issues were resolved. Also, we erred by hiring the wrong consulting company to help with the migrations. That company totally underestimated the effort, complexity, skill sets needed, and schedule. Their project manager was inexperienced, their technical support guy was erratic, they had no methodology or tools, they had no demonstrable experience at our scale, and they had weak executive management support. Our project manager and our team leader both froze like a deer in the headlights, which created a perfect storm.

We learned that some of our customers could not do their work, so we moved them back to the legacy service and halted all new migrations for a year until all 40-plus issues were resolved. We asked the original consultant to stand down, and we brought in Maggie (aka Red Adair) and other talented internal project managers to resurrect the project. I publicly apologized to our customers and took full responsibility for these missteps and the pain and frustration they had caused.

We escalated the service issues to the global company's account representative and her manager, but resolution was light years above their pay grades. Our organization's credibility was shaken, and we desperately needed some serious help to get the necessary attention at the top of that company.

Remembering that two high-ranking former partners at the firm had worked with the senior management team at this global company, I reached out to them for help. One of these partners had hired me 30 years earlier. He was able to quickly connect me with Sandra, the corporate senior vice president responsible for this service. When she called the next day, I said, "We have a five-alarm fire, but we're only getting a one-alarm response from your company. We want and need this service to work. Bad press will not be good for either of our organizations."

She replied, "I can tell you with all confidence that there is the highest level of visibility on your project and absolute commitment to ensure the resolution of all issues and a successful migration. We will do everything possible to remedy the situation, and I am confident we can all be successful together."

Sandra agreed to fund an independent review of the project by a consulting firm dedicated to implementing her company's products and services at scale. This review confirmed the magnitude of the problems on both sides. She funded two field engineers to work with us full time on-site, plus she assigned an additional technical resource to help our team.

Sandra also directed Daniel, an experienced senior product engineer, to work with us to resolve the open technical issues. Daniel brought five product engineers on-site to meet with us and our customers for several days to better understand the issues. These product engineers had never before met a customer out in the wild. Daniel and his team of talented engineers came back several times during the year until they resolved all the open technical issues.

The senior vice president for customer experience at the global company told us that we were the "canary in the coal mine for this service." Well, at this point, we were a swarm of angry birds in their proverbial coal mine. In response, we bought a couple dozen yellow Angry Birds plush toys and gave them out as achievement awards to the staff and customers who persevered with us. It was better to laugh than cry during this painful time.

During the last visit from the engineers, Daniel and I took everyone out for tacos to celebrate (it's a Texas thing). Katie, our technical account manager, said, "Thank you for getting our teams together last night. It was really nice to connect as people as well as teammates, and it felt good to laugh." This global company stepped up, made a significant investment in us, and delivered.

We retained the same independent firm who conducted the review to restart the migrations. They brought proven tools, talented staff, seasoned project managers, and a solid methodology to successfully migrate the rest of our customers. Our project manager, "Red Adair," and the new team leader led the way to restart the migrations.

After the migrations were complete, Daniel sent me this note: "It's been a pleasure working with you for over the past year. While things got off to a rocky start, I appreciate your tenacity and staying with us as we worked through the issues. I'm glad we ended in a good state. Throughout the most challenging times, I really admired you and your team's spirit of this being a partnership and a collaboration. I wish you all the best for the future."

Having a successful strategic vendor partner will help you be more successful. You need to understand what motivates them and must work with them when there is a crisis. Don't hesitate to pull a boss or two—yours or theirs—into the conversation when necessary.

Stay vigilant

Unfortunately, we experienced some bad consultants. Here are the things bad consultants do:

- They waste the client's money or don't treat it like their own.

- They are unresponsive to client requests.

- They never give credit where credit is due.

- They exude an outsized sense of self-importance.

- They take the client executive or their staff for granted.

- They align with one client executive, often the wrong one.

- They bait and switch the proposed consultants without explanation.

- They send inappropriate emails or social media posts.

- They never say "thank you" or "I'm sorry."

- They miss deadlines and go over budget.

These are also the traits of bad employees.

The bottom line is that you should not hesitate to fire a bad consultant. Be on the lookout for these factors, and act before it becomes a crisis. The worst vendors want only your money and always put their interests first, so you have to be vigilant.

One vendor was selected to work on a large project because of the team they proposed. But when the work started, they did not field the proposed team. The entire proposed team was working for another client of the vendor. We learned later that they did not expect to win both projects. They also bid to use a subcontractor with skills and experience in the solution we were implementing. Only one subcontractor resource came to the project on a part-time basis. He was already working on six projects, which was unsustainable. We discovered that they did not even have a teaming agreement in place with the subcontractor, which would have locked in the skilled resources that they bid and that we needed, which is standard operating procedure when proposing to use a subcontractor.

We determined that they wanted only their less-skilled and less-experienced employees working on the project because they made 40% margin on internal resources and only a 15% to 20% margin on subcontractor resources. We replaced the vendor account partner three times, to no avail. The way to ensure that the resource bids are delivered is to add a requirement in your request for proposals that a vendor who does not deliver the proposed team will face severe financial penalties and termination for cause.

This same vendor had the shameless audacity to ask for compensation for work that had not yet started. They claimed 10% to 30% of the work complete on a number of deliverables that, according to their own tracking tool, had not started. We proposed a joint working session, which included our internal auditors, to review each deliverable to determine if any work had been done. Out of 30 deliverables, only four actually had a small percentage of demonstrable work effort. We stopped work and asked them to leave the project site so we would not incur any more costs. Soon, multiple volleys of letters from attorneys were lobbed back and forth and became more strident. The project fell behind, and we ultimately replaced them with another firm. The last vendor account partner was dumb enough to ask me later, "Didn't you agree to give us a good reference?"

My reply was: "Are you crazy? Heck no!"

Demand honesty and integrity

You start from a position of trusting a vendor's sales representative. However, there will be times where they fail to demonstrate honesty and integrity. You will need to demand it.

During the 2008 economic downturn, many software companies created a scheme to allegedly "audit" clients to be certain that all the software being used was properly licensed and maintenance fully paid. This was a revenue-generation gambit well reported in the trade press. My department received an imperious and somewhat threatening letter from one vendor's "software compliance office" in San Diego, California, which said, "I am writing to advise you that XYZ company will be conducting an assessment of your use and deployment of XYZ software in accordance with applicable licensing agreements. XYZ realizes that some customers may wish to resolve known software licensing discrepancies prior to the commencement of the software license review. If this case exists in your organization, please notify our office for assistance in resolving the situation. License and associated maintenance related to software discrepancies should be acquired directly from XYZ."

Our local XYZ account representative, Nathaniel, said this was a compliance issue unrelated to his role in sales. The only problem was that our master agreement with XYZ corporation did not have an audit clause, so we said "no" to the compliance officer who sent the letter. In response, the XYZ compliance officer sent us a copy of an XYZ corporation software agreement dated 10 years prior that had an audit clause. Nonetheless, the person who signed the agreement had no authority from the enterprise to sign, so again we refused to submit to an audit. We learned from other large customers that these so-called audits took a lot of time and energy and that their auditors wanted access to our computing systems, which would not be acceptable to us.

Two months later, a call came into our finance office from an XYZ office in Dallas, Texas. The tone and attitude of the person on the call was threatening and unprofessional. Instead of calling our attorney Steven, they called in error the CFO, who is also named Steven. The XYZ caller was very rude to the CFO's executive assistant, which is never a good idea. She sent me the telephone number, which we discovered belonged to Nathaniel, our local XYZ sales representative. We were not surprised. XYZ backed off on the audit. We reported Nathaniel's unethical behavior to his boss, who assigned a new sales representative who was honest and had integrity.

In another procurement, we sought bids for disaster recovery services. Two leading companies bid. The bids offered similar services and were close in price. During the evaluation, we determined that only one bid included secure data encryption. So we asked ABC corporation to add data encryption, and their bid went up by $50,000. Before we made a formal award to the lower bidder, the ABC sales representative asked one of my direct reports to sign some documents.

My team leader was savvy enough to contact David, who was evaluating the bids. David was still wrapping up the evaluation. It turns out that the sales representative was trying to get a signature before the end of their sales quarter, which was the next day.

My team leader copied me on her response: "I am not sure why you sent this to me, since David has not completed his assessment, and you and I have not talked about this. If I had signed this without much thought, it would have put me in a very awkward situation. I'll be honest: This attempt did not put ABC corporation in a positive light, since it looks like you were trying to close the deal to meet your quarterly sales goal."

The sales rep apologized for the "miscommunication."

Start every relationship from a position of trust. However, when that trust is broken, especially by a vendor, you will need to rectify the situation. That means removing the dishonest party, and sometimes it means finding a new vendor. In either case, the only way the relationship will work is if you both care about each other's success and genuinely work together with honesty and integrity to achieve it.

KEY TAKEAWAYS

- Seek to understand the goals and aspirations of your strategic vendor partners.

- Ensure that your vendors deliver value.

- Genuinely care about the success of your strategic vendor partners, and hold them accountable.

AFTERWORD

THESE STORIES CAME FROM MY OPPORTUNITIES to serve many world-class clients during my 22 years with the firm: The Ohio State University, Columbia University, Vanderbilt University, the University of Michigan, the University of Illinois System, Georgia Tech, the Texas A&M University System, the California State University System, The University of Texas System, the Navajo Nation, government agencies in many states, and several global companies in a variety of industries. I remain friends with many of my former clients and the smart, kind, and generous colleagues at the firm who worked with me over the years and still "think straight and talk straight."

Stories were also gleaned from my eight years serving The University of Texas at Austin, seven of those years as the chief information officer. In 2008, I started working at the university an hour a week, pro bono, to help create the first-ever information technology strategy for the campus. Then I agreed to work half time on the IT strategy beginning in February 2009 and became the interim associate vice president for information technology services in June 2009. President William C. Powers Jr. asked me to serve as the chief information officer in March 2010, which was fun, rewarding, challenging, and sometimes dangerous, just like riding a tiger.

In June 2009, H1N1 swine flu was spreading. President Powers and his leadership team asked if we could move teaching, research, and work online. Unfortunately, the short answer was no. The longer answer: The learning management system was operating on eight- to 10-year-old equipment, and it would be difficult to purchase more during a pandemic. The clunky learning management system software was also buggy, and the external and internal technical support staff were unpredictable. The homegrown student and faculty email system was 18 years old. Students had a maximum of 50 emails at a time; faculty had a maximum of 100 emails at a time. File storage was expensive. And the web technology was 23 years old and supported 2,000 websites, including the university homepage.

Starting in 2009, we began to transition many IT services to off-premise cloud-based products, services, and capabilities. We:

- Collaborated with campus constituencies through newly established IT governance to select state-of-the-art cloud-based email and calendaring services for faculty, students, and staff

- Implemented an innovative cloud-based learning management system, which was selected by the faculty and students

- Added significant cloud-based file storage capabilities at no cost to the faculty, students, or staff

- Deployed a survey tool that met federal security and privacy requirements

- Upgraded the web infrastructure to make it more scalable and to support mobile access; thousands of websites were successfully transitioned to the modern web technical environment

- Provided cloud-based data backup for the faculty and staff

- Migrated to a leading-edge cloud-based human resources and payroll system and launched a platform-as-a-service IT service management tool that reduced multiple ticketing systems to one and included world-class help desk capabilities

In March 2020, when the university decided to go online within two weeks' time due to COVID-19, my successor and his talented team moved mountains in a record amount of time to transition 77,000 people online. In less than two weeks, 52,000 students, 4,000 members of the faculty, and 21,000 staff transitioned to online teaching, learning, research, and work. Kudos to all!

The university has recently updated the IT strategy and will continue with this cloud-first direction. None of this would have been possible without many mutually beneficial and authentic business relationships built and nurtured along the way.

NOTES

CHAPTER 1

1. Robert Greene, *The 48 Laws of Power* (New York: Penguin, 2000).

2. Peter F. Drucker, *Managing Oneself* (Minneapolis: Simply Media, 2008).

3. Naomi Karten, *Managing Expectations: Working with People Who Want More, Better, Faster, Sooner, NOW!* (Boston: Addison-Wesley Professional, 2013).

4. James R. Hagerty, "Robert Vlasic Relied on Jokes to Sell Pickles at Family Firm," *Wall Street Journal*, May 18, 2022, https://www.wsj.com/articles/robert-vlasic-relied-on-jokes-to-sell-pickles-at-family-firm-11652882451.

5. Angela Duckworth, *Grit: The Power of Passion and Perseverance* (New York: Simon & Schuster Audio, 2016).

6. Gary Chapman and Jennifer Thomas, *The Five Languages of Apology: How to Experience Healing in All Your Relationships* (Chicago: Northfield Publishing, 2006).

7. Greene, *48 Laws of Power*.

CHAPTER 2

1. Graham Kenny, "Strategic Planning Should Be a Strategic Exercise," *Harvard Business Review*, October 4, 2022, https://hbr .org/2022/10/strategic-planning-should-be-a-strategic-exercise.

2. Kenny, "Strategic Planning."

3. David J. Collis and Michael G. Rukstad, "Can You Say What Your Strategy Is?" *Harvard Business Review*, April 2008, https:// hbr.org/2008/04/can-you-say-what-your-strategy-is.

4. Karten, *Managing Expectations*.

5. Stephen R. Covey, *The 7 Habits of Highly Effective People* (New York: Free Press, 1989).

6. Covey, *The 7 Habits*.

7. Covey, *The 7 Habits*.

8. Covey, *The 7 Habits*.

9. Covey, *The 7 Habits*.

10. Covey, *The 7 Habits*.

CHAPTER 3

1. William Oncken Jr. and Donald L. Wass, "Management Time: Who's Got the Monkey?" *Harvard Business Review*,

November–December 1999, https://hbr.org/1999/11/management-time-whos-got-the-monkey.

2. Carolyn O'Hara, "What New Team Leaders Should Do First," *Harvard Business Review*, September 11, 2014, https://hbr.org/2014/09/what-new-team-leaders-should-do-first.

3. Michael D. Watkins, *The First 90 Days: Proven Strategies for Getting Up to Speed Faster and Smarter* (Brighton: Harvard Business Review Press, 2013).

4. Watkins, *The First 90 Days.*

5. Kerry Patterson, Joseph Grenny, Ron McMillan, and Al Switzler, *Crucial Conversations: Tools for Talking When the Stakes Are High* (New York: McGraw Hill, 2012).

6. Oncken and Wass, "Who's Got the Monkey?"

7. Chapman and Thomas, *Five Languages of Apology.*

8. Watkins, *The First 90 Days.*

9. Sun Tzu and Ralph D. Sawyer, trans., *The Art of War* (New York: Basic Books, 1994).

10. Jim Collins, *Good to Great: Why Some Companies Make the Leap . . . and Others Don't* (New York: Harper Business, 2001).

11. Jim Collins, "Level 5 Leadership: The Triumph of Humility and Fierce Resolve," *Harvard Business Review*, January 1, 2001, https://hbr.org/2001/01/level-5-leadership-the-triumph-of-humility-and-fierce-resolve-2.

12. Collins, "Level 5 Leadership."

13. Collins, "Level 5 Leadership."

14. "Famous Vince Lombardi Quotes," vincelombardi.com.

15. Kristi Hedges, "5 Questions to Help Your Employees Find Their Inner Purpose," *Harvard Business Review*, August 17, 2017, https://hbr.org/2017/08/5-questions-to-help-your-employees -find-their-inner-purpose.

16. Darrell Rigby, Sarah Elk, and Steve Berez, "Start Stopping Faster," *Harvard Business Review*, September 22, 2020, https:// hbr.org/2020/09/start-stopping-faster#:~:text=Businesses%20 must%20evolve%20to%20match,the%20food%20chain%20 will%20climb.

17. Rigby, Elk, and Berez, "Start Stopping Faster."

18. Rigby, Elk, and Berez, "Start Stopping Faster."

19. Rigby, Elk, and Berez, "Start Stopping Faster."

20. Covey, *The 7 Habits*.

CHAPTER 4

1. Watkins, *The First 90 Days*.

2. Chapman and Thomas, *Five Languages of Apology*.

3. Covey, *The 7 Habits*.

4. Duckworth, *Grit*.

5. *Values. Driven. Leadership: The History of Accenture* (Chantilly, VA: The History Factory, 2005).

6. Christopher Reed, "Red Adair: Swashbuckling Troubleshooter

Renowned for Taming Huge Oil Well Fires, Heading a Business That Carried Out More than 1,000 Missions," *The Guardian*, August 8, 2004, https://www.theguardian.com/news/2004/aug/09/guardianobituaries.usa.

7. *Values. Driven. Leadership.*

8. *Values. Driven. Leadership.*

CHAPTER 5

1. Franklin Covey Company, "Helping Clients Succeed: Business Development Strategy and Skills," 2002, https://resources.franklincovey.com/helping-clients-succeed.

2. Edward Yourdon, *Death March* (Hoboken: Prentice Hall, 1997).

CHAPTER 6

1. Michael Boyles, "Power Mapping: What It Is & How to Use It," *Business Insights* (blog), Harvard Business School Online, July 7, 2022, https://online.hbs.edu/blog/post/power-mapping-what-it-is-and-how-to-use-it.

2. Boyles, "Power Mapping."

ACKNOWLEDGMENTS

FIRST, I WOULD LIKE TO THANK LINDSEY CLARK, my editor at Greenleaf Book Group in Austin, Texas. She helped me create the detailed outline of the book before the COVID-19 pandemic outbreak and was endlessly patient. Without her, this book would not have been possible.

I also want to thank Betsy Busby, who cowrote and edited several hundred weekly blog posts when I was the chief information officer at The University of Texas at Austin. I said to her right before she succumbed to cancer and prior to my retirement from the university in March of 2017, "I need a public relations firm to build my website and establish a social media presence." She paused and said, "Well, my brother Scott has a public relations firm in Los Angeles, The Busby Group."

Betsy and Scott are both extremely talented and are the daughter and son of Horace Busby Jr., Lyndon B. Johnson's speechwriter, consultant, public relations expert, and close confidant. The Busby Group's smart and creative team, Holly, Jian, and Anthony, were pivotal in helping me build my purpose-driven website and establish a relevant social media presence.

Scott Busby also introduced me to Tanya Hall, chief executive officer of Greenleaf Book Group, who wrote *Ideas, Influence, and Income*. Her book was written for me. It inspired me to write my own book. Forty years of my ideas derived from the business world could be shared with people aspiring to grow in their careers. I want to help people hone one of the most important hard skills: creating and nurturing authentic and enduring professional relationships. This book explored how to build a variety of authentic and trusting business relationships, how to keep them, and the consequences of not having them.

ABOUT THE AUTHOR

BRAD ENGLERT is the founder of Brad Englert Advisory and an author, advisor, and technologist. Brad worked for Accenture for 22 years, including 10 years as a partner. He then served The University of Texas at Austin for eight years, including seven years as the chief information officer (CIO).

During Brad's career with Accenture, a global management consulting and technology services firm, he worked in a variety of information technology leadership and operational roles for large, complex institutions of higher education, state governments (Texas, California, Minnesota, Montana), and commercial organizations (Best Buy, Caterpillar, Whirlpool, Bell South, Deutsche Bank, and Wyeth). When Brad retired as a senior partner in 2006, he had a proven track record in information technology operations, large-scale information systems implementations, and strategic planning.

Brad's service to The University of Texas at Austin began in October 2008, as a member of the Strategic Information Technology Advisory Committee. In 2009, he was asked to lead the implementation of the committee's unanimously endorsed recommendations as the chief operating officer of Information Technology Services. He was named CIO in March 2010 and retired in March 2017. He founded Brad Englert Advisory in May 2017.

As CIO, Englert created an information technology governance approach to align strategic capital investments and operating budgets with campus-wide priorities. Englert led a number of transformational initiatives such as transitioning to a modern, cloud-based learning management system, cloud-based email for 52,000 students and tens of thousands of alumni (no ads, no data mining, extra privacy protections), and cloud-based email and calendaring for 4,000 faculty members and 21,000 staff; launching 1,800+ virtual machines; implementing a voice-over-Internet-protocol telephone system (23,000 lines); expanding file sharing capabilities for faculty, students, and staff (100+ terabytes); providing data planning and management resources to researchers; deploying a cloud-based and secure survey tool; investing in the network to support the 300,000+ devices connecting every day; and collaborating with The University of Texas System and the Texas A&M System to upgrade the joint statewide network to 100 gigabytes per second and redundantly connecting the Texas Advanced Computing Center to Internet2 through Dallas and Houston.

Englert's team also built and tested disaster recovery for critical services, upgraded the web infrastructure, developed a mobile strategy, deployed a mobile device responsive home page,

provided data encryption tools, updated the technology road map for supporting teaching and learning, created a master plan for administrative systems modernization, designed and built the new administrative systems technical environment, developed an identity management strategy, offered laptop and workstation data backup capability for all faculty and staff, and transitioned to a cloud-based human resources and payroll solution.

Prior to Accenture, Brad held managerial positions in payroll and human resources and labor relations at the Internal Revenue Service and was a high school teacher in Maitland, New South Wales, Australia. Brad is married to Corliss Hudson Englert. They have two sons, Eric and Nathan.

Brad earned a master's degree in public affairs from The University of Texas at Austin and a bachelor of arts degree in social sciences with honors and distinction from Shimer College, which is now the Shimer Great Books School at North Central College in Naperville, Illinois.